FLORIDA STATE

DAILY DEVOTIONS FOR DIE-HARD FANS

SEMINOLES

FLORIDA STATE

Daily Devotions for Die-Hard Fans: Florida State Seminoles
© 2010 Ed McMinn

Library of Congress Cataloging-in-Publication Data
13 ISBN Digit ISBN: 978-0-9801749-4-6

Manufactured in the United States of America.

Go to http://www.die-hardfans.com for information about other titles in the series.

Cover and interior design by Slynn McMinn.

Every effort has been made to identify copyright holders. Any omissions are wholly unintentional. Extra Point Publishers should be notified in writing immediately for full acknowledgement in future editions.

SEMINOLES

*To the Greater Glory of God
and to Coach Bobby Bowden*

DAY 1

IN THE BEGINNING

Read Genesis 1, 2:1-3.

"God saw all that he had made, and it was very good" (v. 1:31).

While the official records declare that Florida State University first fielded a football team in 1947, they technically are off by almost a half-century.

Established in 1851, West Florida Seminary became Florida State College in 1901. In 1902, a group of students from the college formed a football team. They played for three seasons, wearing purple and gold. Though the records are sketchy, the 1904 squad whipped Stetson 19-6 and a group from the East Florida Seminary at Ocala 23-0. The latter was the forerunner of that school over in Gainesville.

With the passage of the Buckman Act in 1905, the college became the Florida State College for Women. While sports remained a vital part of campus life at Florida State over the next 42 years, that naturally did not include football.

When World War II ended, soldiers came home to Florida "with the G.I. Bill in hand and a college education in their sights." The legislature responded to the flood by reorganizing the women's college into Florida State University in 1947.

The first FSU football team of the modern era took the field against Stetson on Oct. 18, 1947, with a volunteer coach, no scholarship players, no home stadium, and no nickname. Those 45 or

SEMINOLES

so ex-high school players drawn from the ranks of the student body were 0-5 that first season, but three of the losses were by eight points or fewer, including that opener to Stetson 14-6. It didn't take long, however, for the Noles to establishing winning ways. In 1948, the school's new football team was 7-1; FSU was off and running.

Beginnings are important, but what we make of them is even more important. Consider, for example, where the Seminoles have come since that first season. Every morning, you get a gift from God: a new beginning. God hands to you as an expression of divine love a new day full of promise and the chance to right the wrongs in your life. You can use the day to pay a debt, start a new relationship, replace a burned-out light bulb, tell your family you love them, chase a dream, solve a nagging problem . . . or not.

God simply provides the gift. How you use it is up to you. People often talk wistfully about starting over or making a new beginning. God gives you the chance with the dawning of every new day.

You have the chance today to make things right – and that includes your relationship with God.

The most important key to achieving great success is to decide upon your goal and launch, get started, take action, move.
-- John Wooden

Every day is not just a dawn; it is a
precious chance to start over or begin anew.

DAY 2

RAIN CHECK

Read Genesis 9:1-17.

*"I establish my covenant with you: Never again will all
life be cut off by the waters of a flood; never again will
there be a flood to destroy the earth" (v. 11).*

Florida State once came close to having a men's basketball game
rained out.

On the night of Nov. 29, 1994, FSU and South Florida played
under conditions that required ball boys to mop up whatever end
of the court the players weren't on. The Civic Center's patched-up
six-acre roof was leaking.

Mary Ann Lindley noted that a whole crew of ball boys spent
the evening "on hands and knees flipping big white towels across
puddles of water. . . . Some did a kind of rain dance, holding wads
of towel on upright palms to catch falling drops before they splat-
tered on the court." When the players crossed center court, the
ball boys scurried onto the court and proceeded to mop, all the
while warily watching the opposite end in case the teams were
suddenly coming their way. They did their best, but "unsure
footing brought several players to their backsides hard."

Despite the players' discomfiture, the fans who braved the
elements – indoors and out – remained relatively dry unlike a
similar occasion two seasons before when they "put up umbrellas
to avoid rainwater" running from the beams. The two teams
played remarkably well under the circumstances, even managing

a fast-paced game. FSU won 95-88. Taking advantage of the sure footing provided by standing still, FSU's Bob Sura, the school's all-time leading scorer, set a school record by hitting 16 of 16 free throws.

Ironically, that very morning the roofing contractor who would correct the problem permanently had arrived and put his cranes on the roof.

While college basketball games don't often get inconvenienced by rain, for many of your activities, rain is a factor. The kids may be on go for the family picnic; your golf game is set; friends are coming over to grill out -- and then it rains.

Sometimes you make do, but often the rain simply washes away your carefully laid plans. Rain falls when it wants to without checking with you because it answers only to God, who controls the heavens from which it comes, the ground on which it falls, and everything in between.

That includes you, but unlike the rain, God does something rather interesting in your case. While God maintains absolute control over the rain and can do what he will with you – He is God after all -- he lets you choose what controls your life. Choose wisely. Eternity depends upon your choice.

Don't pray when it rains if you don't pray when the sun shines.
-- Pitcher and philosopher Leroy "Satchel" Paige

**While God controls the rain absolutely,
he controls your life only if you choose to let him;
you must choose to surrender to him.**

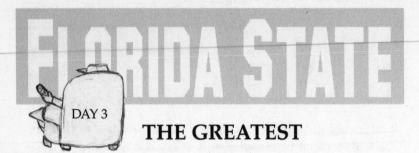

DAY 3

THE GREATEST

Read Mark 9:33-37.

"If anyone wants to be first, he must be the very last, and the servant of all" (v. 35).

Ron Sellers is the greatest receiver in FSU football history. The numbers don't lie.

Offensive records don't often last too long, but though he played from 1966-68, Sellers still holds fourteen FSU receiving records, including receptions for a season and a career, and season and career receiving yards. Nicknamed "Jingle Joints" by a defensive back who said he always looked as though he were about to fly off in different directions, Sellers was a consensus All-America in 1967 and was inducted into the College Football Hall of Fame in 1988.

In 1967, Florida coach Fred Pancoast scouted Notre Dame star Jim Seymour and said to Norm Carlson, Florida's sports information director, "Great speed. He's almost as fast as Sellers." "Hands?" "Fantastic. Almost as good as Sellers." "His moves?" asked Carlson. "Better than any flanker I've ever seen," said Pancoast. "Except, of course, for Sellers." "Are you trying to tell me Sellers is the greatest flanker you've ever seen?" Carlson asked. "Are you kidding?" replied Pancoast. "What would ever make you think anything different?"

Sellers almost didn't get to FSU. The Noles had recruited nine Jacksonville players, but only eight grants-in-aid were mailed;

Sellers was omitted. Head coach Bill Peterson told recruiter John Griner, "That's all we have. Tell the boy we're sorry." But Griner insisted, saying he had given his word. Peterson instructed Griner to find a Xerox machine, make a copy, and tell Sellers he could sign an original later.

Sellers came to FSU, but he never did sign that original.

We all want to be the greatest. The goal for the Noles and their fans every season is the national championship. The competition at work is to be the most productive sales person on the staff or the Teacher of the Year. In other words, we define being the greatest in terms of the struggle for personal success. It's nothing new; Jesus' disciples saw greatness in the same way.

As Jesus illustrated, though, greatness in the Kingdom of God has nothing to do with the world's understanding of success. Rather, the greatest are those who channel their ambition toward the furtherance of Christ's kingdom through love and service, rather than their own advancement, which is a complete reversal of status and values as the world sees them.

After all, who in the world could be greater than the person who has Jesus for a brother and God for a father? And that's every one of us.

My goal was to be the greatest athlete that ever lived.
-- Babe Didrikson Zaharias

**To be great for God has nothing to do
with personal advancement and everything to do
with the advancement of Christ's kingdom.**

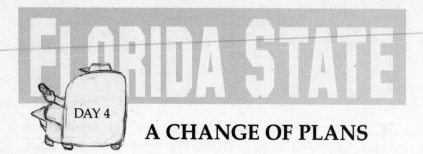

A CHANGE OF PLANS

Read Genesis 18:20-33.

"The Lord said, 'If I find fifty righteous people in the city of Sodom, I will spare the whole place for their sake'" (v. 26).

Originally, the FSU coaches had no plans to use Warrick Dunn on offense, let alone at running back. They quickly changed their plans.

This is the offensive dynamo about whom tackle Todd Fordham said, "He's unreal. Warrick Dunn shows up for big games like no other player in the world." Dunn gained 3,959 yards from 1993-96 to become FSU's all-time leading rusher. "If he weighed 215 pounds," Bobby Bowden once said, "he'd be illegal." Dunn was a three time All-ACC selection whose jersey has been retired.

And yet FSU recruited him as a defensive back. Coach Bowden explained that the team already had Rock Preston out of Miami, and "We didn't have any more offensive scholarships to give. [Defensive coordinator] Mickey [Andrews] had one left and said, 'We'll offer it to that Dunn boy'" down in Louisiana.

So the coaches offered him a defensive back scholarship, which was okay with Dunn. He asked for one concession: Would they give him a chance at tailback? The coaches said yes, but "if we need you at corner, that's where we'll play you."

So one of the greatest running backs in FSU history came to Tallahassee as a defensive back. But in the preseason, injuries to the running backs – including Preston -- forced the coaches to move Dunn up on the depth chart. He lined up at running back for a couple of practices, and FSU's plans for him were changed forever. "It was obvious this guy need[ed] the ball under his arm," Bowden said.

To be unable to adapt to changing circumstances is to stultify and die. It's true of animal life, of business and industry, of the military, of sports teams, of you and your relationships, your job, and your finances.

Changing your plans regularly therefore is rather routine for you. But consider how remarkable it is that the God of the universe may change his mind about something. What could bring that about?

Prayer. Someone -- an old nomad named Abraham or a 21st-century FSU fan like you -- talks to God, who listens and considers what is asked of him.

You may feel uncomfortable praying. Maybe you're reluctant and embarrassed; perhaps you feel you're not very good at it. But nobody majors in prayer at school, and as for being reluctant, what have you got to lose? Your answer may even be a change of plans on God's part. Such is the power of prayer.

I've always asked for good health, wisdom, and for help in trying to be good. I definitely believe in prayer.
-- Bobby Bowden

Prayer is so powerful it may even change God's mind.

DAY 5

JUST PERFECT

Read Matthew 5:43-48.

"Be perfect, therefore, as your heavenly Father is perfect"
(v. 48).

For years, Bobby Bowden kept an empty picture frame in his office. Finally, after his 34th season as a head coach, he got a picture for it.

The photograph was of the 1999 national champions because Bowden had been reserving that frame for his first undefeated team. Those 12-0 Seminoles were actually the second team in FSU football history to go undefeated. In the first year the Tribe moved into Doak Campbell Stadium and only the fourth year of football in the modern era, the 1950 squad went 8-0. The head coach was Don Veller, who compiled a record of 31-12-1 from 1948-52 and laid the foundation for FSU's move into big-time football. The 1950 team defeated Troy State, Randolph-Macon, Howard, Newberry, Sewanee, Stetson in the first game in Doak Campbell, Mississippi College, and Tampa.

Forty-nine years later, playing this time on the biggest stage college football has, the Seminoles went undefeated again, holding the top ranking every week of the season. The national champs had some Saturday laughers, blasting Louisiana Tech, North Carolina State, North Carolina, Duke, Wake Forest, Virginia, and Maryland. They also had some nail-biters, outscoring Georgia Tech 41-35, whipping Miami 31-21 after falling behind 21-14, nudging Clemson 17-14 though Tommy Bowden's Tigers led 14-3 at the half, and clipping Florida 30-23 after the Gators led 16-13 at the break.

The season every fan dreams about ended in the Sugar Bowl with a 46-29 win over Virginia Tech and quarterback Michael Vick. Bowden had his perfect season and his photograph.

Nobody's perfect; we all make mistakes every day. We botch our personal relationships despite repeatedly trying to get them right. At work we seek competence, not perfection. To insist upon personal or professional perfection in our lives is to set the bar so impossibly high that physical, emotional, and mental meltdowns are inevitable.

Yet that is exactly the standard God sets for us in our relationships with others. Our love is to be perfect, without hesitation, without interruption, without conditions -- just the way God loves us. But since we're only human, aren't we being set up for failure?

Yes, it's an impossible standard for us, this idea of loving perfectly as God does, but God nevertheless expects us to do our best and never quit trying. And in his perfect love for us, God makes allowance for our imperfect love and the consequences of it. We call him Jesus.

I think many Christians make a mistake. Nobody's perfect.
                                                      -- Bobby Bowden

**In his perfect love for us, God provides a way
for us to escape the consequences
of our imperfect love for him: Jesus.**

DAY 6

THE BIG TIME

Read Matthew 2:19-23.

"He went and lived in a town called Nazareth" (v. 23).

One game more than any other singlehandedly propelled Florida State football from the backwoods to the big time.

It seems ludicrous to even attempt to determine the biggest game in Seminole football history because FSU has had so many of them. But Lee Corso, who starred for the Seminoles from 1953-56, once said, "I think that 10-0 win over Tennessee in Knoxville in 1958 was the biggest game in Florida State football."

This was a time when FSU's history as an all-girls school was still so recent Seminole football players were frequently needled about it. The football program was only eleven years old. With the exception of N.C. State, midway through the 1958 season, the Noles were 0-14 against the established programs such as Auburn, Georgia, Miami, and Georgia Tech.

Exactly what the football world thought of Florida State's football program at the time was perhaps best revealed by Tennessee coach Bowden Wyatt. FSU coach Tom Nugent conducted a clinic on the passing game that Wyatt attended. Nugent rightfully took pride in his meticulous playing field, but Wyatt disdainfully remarked, "We don't grow beautiful grass at Tennessee. We just teach great football."

On Oct. 25, 1958, the 4-2 Seminoles went into Knoxville and stunned the Vols in a game Corso described as "monumental" and "earthshaking." Why was it so important? "That was the first win over a Southeastern Conference team," said Corso, "the first over a program people recognized as a major power. After that, we had legitimacy in the South."

The Seminoles had moved up to the big time.

It's a move we often desire to make in our own lives. Bumps in the road, one stoplight communities, and towns with only a service station, a church, and a voting place litter the American countryside. Maybe you were born in one of them and grew up in a virtually unknown village in a backwater county. Perhaps you started out on a stage far removed from the bright lights of Broadway, the glitz of Hollywood, or the halls of power in Washington, D.C.

Those original circumstances don't have to define or limit you, though, for life is much more than geography. It is about character and walking with God whether you're in the countryside or the city.

Jesus knew the truth of that. After all, he grew up in a small town in an inconsequential region of an insignificant country ruled by foreign invaders.

Where you are doesn't matter. What you are does.

I am living proof that it doesn't matter where you come from; if you turn your life over to God, He will do unbelievable things.

-- Bobby Bowden

**Where you live may largely be the culmination
of a series of circumstances; what you are
is a choice you make.**

DAY 7

THE SURE FOUNDATION

Read Luke 6:46-49.

"I will show you what he is like who comes to me and hears my words and puts them into practice. He is like a man building a house, who dug down deep and laid the foundation on rock" (vv. 47-48).

Championship sports programs just don't suddenly appear. They are built, which requires a solid foundation. The foundation for today's successful softball program at FSU was laid by the slow-pitch national champions of 1981 and 1982.

Virtually forgotten amid today's high-profile, fast-pitch NCAA championship is the 1981 team, which won the first national championship in Florida State women's athletics history. Playing under the auspices of the defunct AIAW, the Seminoles were 54-7 in 1981, closing the season with 16 straight wins, going undefeated in the national championship tournament, and whipping North Carolina 4-1 for the title.

Shortstop Darby Cottle and second baseman Jan Sikes were named All-America. Sikes hit .477 for the season.

Everything was in place for another great season in 1982, and the Seminoles responded with a 56-10 record and their second straight national championship. The Noles were virtually unchallenged in the championship tournament as they outscored their opponents 46-6 before meeting the Florida Gators in the finals. They added to their 8-6 edge in the series by winning 9-4.

Cottle was named the AIAW Player of the Year and was joined on the All-America team by Natalie Drouin, Susan Painter, Toni Robinette, and Sikes.

In 1984, the AIAW was disbanded in favor of the NCAA, but "the players on those [1981 and 1982] teams were the founders of a legacy that continues today." They laid the foundation.

Like FSU's entire athletics program, your life is an ongoing project, a work in progress. As with any complex construction job, if your life is to be stable, it must have a solid foundation, which holds everything up and keeps everything together.

R. Alan Culpepper said in *The New Interpreter's Bible*, "We do not choose whether we will face severe storms in life; we only get to choose the foundation on which we will stand." In other words, tough times are inevitable.

If the foundation upon which your life is built isn't rock-solid, you will have nothing on which to stand as those storms buffet you, nothing to keep your life from flying apart into a cycle of disappointment and destruction.

But when the foundation is solid and sure, you can take the blows, stand strong, recover, and live with joy and hope. Only one foundation is foolproof: Jesus Christ. Everything else you build upon will fail you.

First master the fundamentals.

-- Larry Bird

In the building of your life, you must start with a foundation in Jesus Christ, or the first trouble that shows up will knock you down.

CHEAP TRICKS

Read Acts 19:11-20.

"The evil spirit answered them, 'Jesus I know, and I know about Paul, but who are you?'" (v. 15)

There are trick plays and there are trick plays. And then there is the "puntrooskie."

College football analyst Beano Cook called it "the best play since *My Fair Lady*." It debuted on Sept. 17, 1988, against the third-ranked Clemson Tigers. Sports writer Gary Long declared, "'Puntrooskie' will reign forever as the boldest and riskiest of the multitude of trick plays Bobby Bowden's Florida State football teams have attempted."

The puntrooskie was at heart just a glorified fake punt; what set it apart were the circumstances under which it was pulled off. Had it failed, FSU would almost surely have lost the game. The tenth-ranked Noles faced fourth down at their own 21 with only 1:33 left to play in a 21-21 game and lined up in punt formation. The deception began when center David Willingham snapped the ball to the upback, Dayne Williams, and not to the punter, Tim Corlew. who leaped as if the ball had sailed over his head and then took off in frantic pursuit.

Williams caught the snap, stepped quickly behind blocking back LeRoy Butler, an All-American cornerback as a senior in 1989, and slipped the ball between Butler's legs. Butler counted to three without moving while Williams headed around right end,

SEMINOLES

following a convoy of pulling guards.

The left sideline lay wide open for Butler, who scampered seventy-eight yards to the Clemson one. After a touchdown was nullified, the Seminoles kicked a field goal for the 24-21 win. FSU would go undefeated the rest of the season and finish ranked third.

Scam artists are everywhere — and they love trick plays. An e-mail encourages you to send money to some foreign country to get rich. That guy at your front door offers to resurface your driveway at a ridiculously low price. A TV ad promises a pill to help you lose weight without diet or exercise.

You've been around; you check things out before deciding. The same approach is necessary with spiritual matters, too, because false religions and bogus Christian denominations abound. The key is what any group does with Jesus. Is he the son of God, the ruler of the universe, and the only way to salvation? If not, then what the group espouses is something other than the true Word of God.

The good news about Jesus does indeed sound too good to be true. But the only catch is that there is no catch. No trick -- just the truth.

When you run trick plays and they work, you're a genius. But when they don't work, folks question your sanity.

-- Bobby Bowden

God's promises through Jesus sound too good to be true, but the only catch is that there is no catch.

BLIND JUSTICE

Read Micah 6:6-8.

"He has showed you, O man, what is good. And what does the Lord require of you? To act justly and to love mercy and to walk humbly with your God" (v. 8).

What happened to the Seminoles against Florida in the 1966 game was a crime.

In the third game of his Heisman-Trophy season, Steve Spurrier had the Gators with a 22-19 lead. But with only 28 seconds left, Seminole quarterback Gary Pajcic launched a 45-yard bomb to the end zone toward tight end Lane Fenner. Writer Gary Long said that photographs in the Sunday edition of the *Tallahassee Democrat* "showed Fenner in-bounds with apparent control of the football." The field judge, however, "who will live in infamy at FSU," ruled Fenner juggled the ball as he went out of bounds. The result was no catch, no touchdown, and a Florida victory.

T.K. Wetherell, who was in the pass pattern on the play, had no doubts that the Noles were robbed. "I don't mind them stealing it," he said. "I just wish they'd admit it."

According to author Julian Clarkson, one former Gator student did confess to the reality of the awful injustice done the Seminoles. The student supposedly needled an FSU fan by saying, "You're right. He was in [bounds], and we stole it from you. That makes it even sweeter." The speaker was Florida's governor at the time, Lawton Chiles.

Wetherell said he had seen the quote and remarked, "I'm surprised they didn't use that against him in the [gubernatorial] campaign. Somebody ought to have gone out to the game and handed out fliers with that on it. It would have cost him 100,000 votes."

Where's the justice when cars fly past you just as a state trooper pulls you over? When a con man swindles an elderly neighbor? When crooked politicians treat your tax dollars as their personal slush fund? When children starve?

Injustice enrages us, but anger is not enough. The establishment of justice in this world has to start with each one of us. The Lord requires it of us. For most of us, a just world is one in which everybody gets what he or she deserves.

But that is not God's way. God expects us to be just and merciful in all our dealings without consideration as to whether the other person "deserves" it. The justice we dispense should truly be blind.

If that doesn't sound "fair," then pause and consider that when we stand before God, the last thing we want is what we deserve. We want mercy, not justice.

None of us wants justice from God. What we want is mercy because if we got justice, we'd all go to hell.

-- Bobby Bowden

**God requires that we dispense justice and mercy
without regards to deserts, exactly what we pray
we will in turn receive from God.**

PROMISES, PROMISES

Read 2 Corinthians 1:16-20.

"No matter how many promises God has made, they are 'Yes' in Christ" (v. 20).

Bobby Bowden kept a promise he made even when it cost him a quarterback recruit. He wound up getting a Heisman-Trophy winner who led the Noles to the 1999 national championship.

On Jan. 21, 1991, Bowden wrote a letter to Chris Weinke, who had packed up and left campus just four days after arriving in Tallahassee. A $600,000 bonus from baseball's Toronto Blue Jays was just too much for Weinke to ignore. Convinced of Weinke's ability, Bowden told him that if baseball didn't work out, he could come back and quarterback the Seminoles.

"I never expected to hear from him again," Bowden said. But six years later, quarterbacks coach Mark Richt said to his head coach, "Guess who I heard from? Chris Weinke wants to come back." The immediate concern was whether Weinke was too old, whether he still had his legs. Richt then voiced another concern: If they took Weinke back, they would lose a valued recruit, Drew Henson.

The two coaches talked it over and agreed that a promise had been made and should be kept even if it cost them Henson. Thus, not offering Weinke a scholarship was never a serious consideration. Bowden told Weinke, "I made a promise to you, and you're more than welcome to come back. We're not guaranteeing anything, but we'd love to have you back."

Drew Henson wound up at Michigan, and in January 1997, 24-year-old freshman Chris Weinke enrolled at FSU and began his now legendary football career.

All because Bobby Bowden kept an old promise.

One of life's most basic truths is that the promises you make to others don't say much about you; the promises you keep, however, tell everything about you.

The promise to your daughter to be there for her softball game. To your son to help him with his math homework. To your parents to come see them soon. To your spouse to remain faithful until death parts you. And do you even remember what you promised God that night you were in so much trouble?

You may carelessly throw promises around, but you can never outpromise God, who is downright profligate with his promises. For instance, he has promised to love you always, to forgive you no matter what you do, and to prepare a place for you with him in Heaven.

And there's more good news in that God operates on this simple premise: Promises made are promises kept. You can rely absolutely on God's promises.

The people to whom you make them should be able to rely just as surely on your promises.

In the everyday pressures of life, I have learned that God's promises are true.

-- Major leaguer Garret Anderson

God steadfastly keeps his promises just as those who rely on you expect you to keep yours.

DAY 11

NO RESPECT

Read Mark 8:31-38.

"He then began to teach them that the Son of Man must suffer many things and be rejected by the elders, chief priests and teachers of the law, and that he must be killed" (v. 31).

You would think the player who had the greatest single game in NCAA baseball history would merit a little respect from major-league scouts – but not FSU's Marshall McDougall.

On May 9, 1999, against Maryland, junior McDougall did something that FSU coach Mike Martin said "rivals the 100 points Wilt Chamberlain scored in one game. What Marshall did will never be done again unless they move the fence right behind the infield." What Marshall did in the 26-2 rout was hit six home runs, drive in 16 runs, and total 25 bases – NCAA records all.

McDougall finished that 1999 season hitting .419 with 28 homers and 106 RBIs. He was first-team All-America and the Most Outstanding Player at the College World Series.

After his sensational season, McDougall was told repeatedly by the scouts that he would be drafted between the fourth and the tenth rounds. On draft day, though, 798 players were selected before the Boston Red Sox deigned to take him in the 26th round. The Red Sox were so unimpressed with McDougall that they didn't even offer him a signing bonus.

Perplexed by the draft and Boston's lack of respect for

SEMINOLES

McDougall, Martin called the whole business "one of the biggest surprises I've seen. You can't have a year like Marshall had last year and be an average baseball player. This guy's special."

McDougall returned to FSU for his senior season, was drafted by the Oakland A's in the ninth round of the 2000 draft, and made his major-league debut in June 2005.

Rodney Dangerfield made a good living as a comedian with a repertoire that was really only countless variations on one punch line: "I don't get no respect." Dangerfield was successful because he struck a chord with his audience. No one wants to be perceived by others as being worthy of only a late-round draft pick and no signing bonus. You want the respect, the honor, the esteem, and the regard that you feel you've earned.

But more often than not, you don't get it. Still, you shouldn't feel too badly; you're in good company. In the ultimate example of disrespect, Jesus – the very Son of God -- was arrested, bound, scorned, ridiculed, struck, spit upon, tortured, condemned, and executed.

As incredible as it sounds, God allowed his son to undergo such treatment because of his high regard and his love for you. You are respected by almighty God! Could anyone else's respect really matter?

Play for your own self-respect and the respect of your teammates.
-- Vanderbilt coach Dan McGugin

**You may not get the respect you deserve,
but at least nobody's driving nails into you
as they did to Jesus.**

ANIMAL MAGNETISM

Read Psalm 139:1-18.

*"For you created my inmost being; you knit me together
in my mother's womb. I praise you because I am fearfully
and wonderfully made" (vv. 13-14).*

It has been called "perhaps the most spectacular tradition in all
of college football."

"It" is the heartpounding moment when Chief Osceola charges
onto Bobby Bowden Field at Doak Campbell Stadium riding an
Appaloosa horse named Renegade. When he plants that flaming
spear at midfield, the fan frenzy becomes palpable. "You're
starting the fire underneath the team and the fans," said an FSU
student who served as Chief Osceola. "It's an incredible adren-
aline rush. You have fifteen hundred pounds of an animal underneath you, and he's ready to charge."

The tradition was born on Sept. 16, 1978, against Oklahoma State
(which the Seminoles won 38-20). The idea was the brainstorm of
businessman Bill Durham when he was a student working on the
homecoming committee in 1962 and was trying to come up with
a way to get students and other fans fired up about the team. "At
that time, people didn't even as a large group wear garnet and
gold," Durham remembered. The administration didn't like the
idea, though, so it died until years later Bobby Bowden and his
wife, Ann, embraced the concept.

In an age of political correctness, the Seminole mascot has

SEMINOLES

drawn some criticism as a demeaning stereotype, but Durham said Chief Osceola and Renegade are exactly the opposite. The Seminole Tribe's chief originally granted permission to use the mascot; the tribe helped design the first costume. "It's a salute to the determination of the Seminole Indians," Durham said.

It certainly makes for one of the most electrifying moments in college sports.

Animals such as Renegade elicit our awe and our respect. Nothing enlivens a trip more than glimpsing turkeys, bears, or deer in the wild. Admit it: You go along with the kids' trip to the zoo because you think it's a cool place too. All that variety of life is mind-boggling. Who could conceive of an Appaloosa, a walrus, a moose, or a prairie dog? Who could possibly have that rich an imagination?

But the next time you're in a crowd, look around at the parade of faces. Who could come up with the idea for all those different people? For that matter, who could conceive of you? You are unique, a masterpiece who will never be duplicated.

The master creator, God Almighty, is behind it all. He thought of you and brought you into being. If you had a manufacturer's label, it might say, "Lovingly handmade in Heaven by #1 -- God."

Chief Osceola and Renegade are the most wonderful tradition in college football.
-- FSU Alumni Association associate director Betty Lou Joanos

You may consider some painting or a magnificent animal a work of art, but the real creative masterpiece is you.

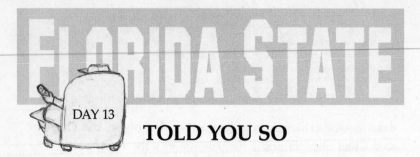

DAY 13

TOLD YOU SO

Read Matthew 24:15-31.

"See, I have told you ahead of time" (v. 25).

Brad Scott could certainly be forgiven for telling his boss, Bobby Bowden, "I told you so," especially after Bowden threatened to shoot him if he were wrong.

In the 1985 game against Nebraska in Lincoln, FSU led 17-13 as the clock ticked down in this battle between top-ten teams. Scott, the tight ends coach, recalled that FSU got the ball. "We had the game won," Scott said, meaning the Noles could take a knee and run out the clock.

But Bowden didn't think so and wanted to run plays. Scott dared to speak out, insisting FSU had the game won, that they should just take a knee until the clock ran out. "Are you sure on this?" Bowden asked. "Are you sure?" Scott replied that he was sure.

Scott recalled that Billy Smith, the Florida highway patrolman in charge of Bowden's security, was as usual standing beside the coach. Bowden looked at Scott and said, "Brad, if you are wrong, I'm going to take that gun of Bill's and shoot you."

Scott remembered that Smith's eyes got real big. A suddenly rattled Scott took a step or two away from Bowden and got on the phone to offensive coordinator Wayne McDuffie. "Hey, McDuffie," I'm right, ain't I?" Scott asked.

He was right. The Noles ran out the clock, and the young coach got a big hug from Bowden after the game. "That's the way to be on top of it," Bowden said. Scott let the chance pass to say "I told you so."

Don't you just hate it in when somebody says, "I told you so"? That means the other person was right and you were wrong; that other person has spoken the truth. You could have listened to that know-it-all in the first place, but then you would have lost the chance yourself to crow, "I told you so" -- and you just couldn't pass that up.

In our pluralistic age and society, many so-called "good" people view truth as relative' in their worldview, absolute truth does not exist. No one has a monopoly on the truth; all belief systems have equal value and merit. We just have to find the one that best suits us and makes us feel good about ourselves.

But this is a ghastly, dangerous fallacy of hubris and convenience because it disdains the truth that God proclaimed in the presence and the words of Jesus. In speaking the truth, Jesus told everybody exactly what he was going to do: come back and take his faithful with him. Those who don't listen or who don't believe will be left behind with those four awful words, "I told you so," ringing in their ears and wringing their souls.

There's nothing in this world more instinctively abhorrent to me than finding myself in agreement with my fellow humans.
-- Lou Holtz

Jesus matter-of-factly told us what he has planned:
He will return to gather all the faithful to himself.

DIVIDED LOYALTIES

Read Matthew 6:1-24.

"No one can serve two masters" (v. 24a).

Walter Dix was loyal to FSU even when it meant turning down millions of dollars.

Everyone expected Dix to turn pro after he ran two of the fastest times in the world in 2007 as a Seminole junior. He had a six-year, $6 million offer on the table, plus, Dix said, "My friends, most of them, say go pro." But Dix made his own decision, and ultimately his loyalty to FSU won out over the fast bucks. Dix wanted to graduate.

But there was another reason he came back for his senior season. As he put it, "I don't care about signing a deal. I have a uniform to run with." That was the same reason he turned down another lucrative offer before the Olympic trials in July 2008. He wanted to run in that garnet and gold uniform.

And run he did. Dix led the Seminoles to a third straight NCAA track and field national title in 2008, winning a third 200m championship. He finished his storied career with 18 All-America honors and six individual outdoor national championships. Dix was the only American to qualify for both the 100m and the 200m dashes for the Beijing Olympics. He then won bronze medals in both events.

About that big contract Dix turned down to return to FSU? Shortly after his performance at the Olympic trials, Dix signed

SEMINOLES

what was called "a record-breaking deal" with Nike, said to be for seven figures. Walter Dix stuck by his convictions, including loyalty to FSU, and it paid off for him.

Florida State or his immediate professional career: Walter Dix had to decide where his loyalty lay. You probably understand the stress that comes with divided loyalties such as those Dix faced. The Christian work ethic drives you to be successful. The world, however, often makes demands and presents images that conflict with your devotion to God: movies deride God; couples play musical beds in TV sitcoms; and TV dramas portray Christians as killers following God's orders.

Even more directly in your own life, it's Sunday morning and the office will be quiet or the golf course won't be crowded. What do you do when your heart and loyalties are pulled in two directions?

Jesus knew of the struggle we face; that's why he spoke of not being able to serve "two masters." We will inevitably, he pointed out, wind up serving one master and despising the other. Put in terms of either serving God or despising God, the choice is stark and clear.

Your loyalty is to God -- always.

I am the most loyal player money can buy.
-- Former major leaguer Don Sutton

God does not condemn you for being successful
and enjoying popular culture, but your loyalty
must lie first and foremost with him.

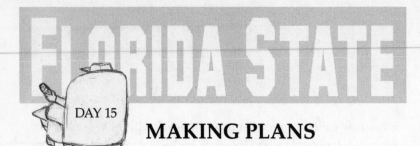

MAKING PLANS

Read Psalm 33:1-15.

"The plans of the Lord stand firm forever, the purposes of his heart through all generations" (v. 11).

When Bobby Bowden came to Tallahassee in 1976, he found a mess that threatened to kill the football program and a plan that threatened to make his career exceedingly brief.

The Seminoles had gone 0-11, 1-10 and 3-8 the three seasons before Bowden's arrival. The program was in such a sorry state that, according to Bowden, "the stadium seated 41,000 and we were averaging 17,000 fans per game." As a result, the athletic department was deep in debt.

Prior to Bowden's arrival, athletic director John Bridgers had devised a unique plan to get some money into the Tallahassee coffers. He scheduled some of the nation's most storied programs on the road for the big paydays they offered. Rick Reilly of *Sports Illustrated* said Bridgers "would've scheduled the Kremlin if the rubles were right."

Bridgers then turned the killer schedule over to Bowden, who looked at it and said, "No way a guy can survive that thing." The ten-year run included road games against Nebraska, LSU, Ohio State, Michigan, Arizona State, and Notre Dame. Bridgers' strategy reached its zenith in 1981 when the Seminoles played Nebraska, Ohio State, Notre Dame, Pittsburgh, and LSU on successive weekends, all on the road. But the Noles won three of the five. They beat Nebraska 18-14 in 1980, a game Bowden said drew national attention to Florida State, swept Ohio State, beat Notre Dame, won three from Arizona State, and whipped LSU four times.

Ultimately, an innovative and desperate plan yielded not only money but a national reputation.

Successful living takes planning, You go to college to improve your chances for a better paying job. You use blueprints to build your home. You plan for retirement. You carefully map out your vacation to have the most fun and maximize the limited time you have available. You even plan your children -- sometimes.

All your plans nevertheless amount to little more than calculated finger-crossing because they can all be laid waste overnight, often by circumstances beyond your control. The world insists upon proceeding without deferring to your precious plans.

You can, however, plan with absolute certainty that which really matters in your life. That is, you can ensure that your life is rich with joy, love, peace, kindness, gentleness, and faithfulness.

That's exactly the kind of life God has planned for you, and God is ready and willing to serve as your life's planning partner. God's plans for your life are not only a sure thing – they are eternal.

If you don't know where you are going, you will wind up somewhere else.

-- Yogi Berra

Your plans may ensure a successful life;
God's plans will ensure a successful eternity.

DAY 16

GOOD SPORTS

Read Titus 2:1-8.

"Show integrity, seriousness and soundness of speech that cannot be condemned, so that those who oppose you may be ashamed because they have nothing bad to say about us" (vv. 7b, 8).

An FSU football player's boorish act sparked the creation of a unique symbol of sportsmanship.

Ed Jonas, one of the nation's leading portrait artists and an FSU graduate, was watching a game when a Seminole player struck a Heisman-Trophy pose after making a big play. The act disappointed Jonas, who saw it as another example of the poor sportsmanship that had come to pervade the college game.

Rather than just excoriating his alma mater with a letter to the editor, Jonas was inspired by his disgust to create a statue dedicated to sportsmanship. On Nov. 18, 2000, before the Florida game, *Sportsmanship* was unveiled. The 15-feet by 14-feet tableau, the largest in Tallahassee, depicts one football player helping up a fallen foe. The players, which are eleven feet tall, are on a granite and concrete base in the Al Strum Plaza on the south side of FSU's University Center.

Jonas was a varsity gymnast for the Seminoles, so he understood the absolute necessity for sportsmanship in collegiate competition. "Your agility, quickness, and athletic talent fall by the wayside as you age," he once said. "Only the seeds of class and respect for yourself and your opponents endure. I don't know if the statue will make a difference, but if it influences one or two people it will be worth it."

The statue resulted from collaboration between Jonas and the Seminole boosters and a gift from Margaret Strum Allesee, a cheerleader on FSU's first squad in 1947 and the first woman to win a varsity letter at FSU.

One of life's paradoxes is that many who would never consider cheating on the tennis court or the racquetball court to gain an advantage think nothing of doing so in other areas of their life. In other words, the good sportsmanship they practice on the golf course or even on the Monopoly board doesn't carry over. They play with the truth, cut corners, abuse others verbally, run rough-shod over the weaker, and generally cheat whenever they can to gain an advantage on the job or in their personal relationships.

But good sportsmanship is a way of living, not just of playing. Shouldn't you accept defeat without complaint (You don't have to like it.); win gracefully without gloating; treat your competition with fairness, courtesy, generosity, and respect? That's the way one team treats another in the name of sportsmanship. That's the way one person treats another in the name of Jesus.

One person practicing sportsmanship is better than a hundred teaching it.
                                                            -- Knute Rockne

Sportsmanship -- treating others with courtesy, fairness, and respect -- is a way of living, not just a way of playing.

DAY 17

TOP SECRET

Read Romans 2:1-16.

"This will take place on the day when God will judge men's secrets through Jesus Christ, as my gospel declares" (v. 16).

Imagine being so secretive about some of the plays for a game that you don't even tell your *players* about them – but that was Bobby Bowden's policy.

The unusually secretive approach resulted from a lesson Bowden learned against Florida in 1983. The coaches introduced an offensive package the week of the game that included some trick plays Bowden was convinced would be crucial to a win in Gainesville.

So the first time the Noles tried their new offensive set, the Gators moved right into a defense that shut the play down. That happened all afternoon long. "They knew exactly what we were going to do," Bowden said. The new formation was a complete failure.

Only years later did Bowden learn what had happened, and his source was a Florida coach who kidded him about it. One of the Seminole players, excited about the plays, had told his father, "Daddy, we're going to do this tomorrow, and you're going to see me do this. They don't know we're going to do it."

The dad just happened to be at a party in Gainesville that night, and he tipped a friend off to watch for what his son would be doing in the game. A Gator fan overheard the conversation and passed the secret information on to the Florida coaches.

After that, Bowden often urged his coaches to "Don't tell the kids," so they wouldn't know that some special plays were part of the game plan until they were called in the game.

As Bobby Bowden was about some of his football plays, you have to be vigilant about the personal information you prefer to keep secret. Much information about you—from credit reports to what movies you rent—is readily available. In our information age, people you don't know may know a lot about you, or at least they can find out. And some of them may use this information for harm.

Due diligence may well allow you to be reasonably successful in keeping some secrets from the world at large, but you should never deceive yourself into believing you are keeping secrets from God. God knows everything about you, including the things you wouldn't want proclaimed at church. All your sins, mistakes, failures, shortcomings, quirks, prejudices, and desires – God knows all your would-be secrets.

But here's something God hasn't kept a secret: No matter what he knows about you, he loves you still.

Coaches steal ideas from one another all the time. There ain't any secrets in coaching.

– Bobby Bowden

You have no secrets before God, and it's no secret in return that he loves you nevertheless.

DAY 18

HEART AND SOUL

Read Romans 12:1-2.

"Therefore, I urge you, brothers, in view of God's mercy, to offer your bodies as living sacrifices, holy and pleasing to God – this is your spiritual act of worship" (v. 1).

Linebacker Daryl Bush was so committed to FSU football that he earned the nicknames "Psycho" and "Death Row."

Ken Alexander and Alonzo Horner dubbed Bush "Death Row" in the summer of 1993. "He looked and played like a guy who was on death row with two weeks to live and didn't care about anything," said Alexander. Bush was a brooding introvert who, when he hit the field, transformed into "a type A gridiron madman, replete with screams and yells and helmet pounding." Thus, the nickname "Psycho."

Bush was a third-team All-American middle linebacker in 1997 and a first-team Academic All-America in 1996. He was the team's leading tackler in 1997 and in 1994 as a redshirt freshman; three times he was second-team All-ACC.

The depth of his commitment separated Bush from other players. In the Noles' 34-16 win over Miami in 1996, Bush suffered a concussion from a massive collision he instigated. His first question after his head cleared was "How's the other guy?" Only when he was assured that "the other guy" was out of the game did Bush agree to stay on the sidelines.

During a preseason scrimmage in 1995, he suffered a ligament tear but refused to sit. He missed only three games that season, having his knee drained each week. That impressed Bobby Bowden, who compared Bush's commitment to that of athletes of past decades.

Daryl Bush gave FSU football his heart and soul.

When you stood in a church and recited your wedding vows, did you make a decision that you could walk away from when things got tough or did you make a lifelong commitment? Is your job just a way to get a paycheck, or are you committed to it?

Commitment seems almost a dirty word in our society these days, a synonym for *chains*, an antonym for *freedom*. Perhaps this is why so many people are afraid of Jesus: Jesus demands commitment. To speak of offering yourself as "a living sacrifice" is not to speak blithely of making a decision but of heart-body-mind-and-soul commitment.

But commitment actually means "purpose and meaning," especially when you're talking about your life. Commitment makes life worthwhile. Anyway, in insisting upon commitment, Jesus isn't asking anything from you that he hasn't already given you himself. His commitment to you was so deep that he died for you.

I tell my players, 'If I have your faith, trust, and commitment, we will win a lot of games.' I think God is looking for the same ingredients in each of us.

-- *Bobby Bowden*

**Rather than constraining you, commitment
to Jesus lends meaning to your life,
releasing you to move forward with purpose.**

DAY 19

THE BEAUTIFUL PEOPLE

Read Matthew 23:23-28.

"Woe to you, teachers of the law and Pharisees, you hypocrites! You are like whitewashed tombs, which look beautiful on the outside, but on the inside are full of dead men's bones and everything unclean" (v. 27).

It's official. When she was at FSU, Gabrielle Reece was one of the five most beautiful women in the world. *Elle* magazine said so.

Reece was once described rather flatteringly as "arguably the most famous female athlete of all." She's certainly famous among Seminole fans; in 1997 she was inducted into the Florida State Athletics Hall of Fame. She is one of FSU's greatest volleyball players ever. During her career from 1987-90, she set the Seminole record for solo blocks (career and season) and the career record for total blocks. She led the league in kills all four years. She was All-Metro Conference in '89 and '90 and went on to play professionally.

But it was the other career that began while Reece was at FSU for which she is most recognized. In 1989, she began her modeling career, which launched her as an international celebrity. She said later in a book that while she was at FSU she was "very alone," resented by other players "because she would model in the spring while the others trained for the fall." Those other players certainly couldn't question her commitment to the team or to volleyball. She once turned down a two-day modeling job that paid $35,000 because she had a match.

As *Elle* declared in 1989, Gabrielle Reece is one of the beautiful people. She never left the athletic roots she laid down at FSU, though, noting in her book her perturbation over the fact that most people recognize her as a model first and a volleyball player second.

Remember the brunette who sat behind you in history class? Or the blonde in English? Maybe it was Gabrielle Reece, whom you didn't recognize at the time. And how about that hunk from the next apartment who washes his car every Saturday morning?

We do love those beautiful people.

It is worth remembering amid our adulation of superficial beauty that *Elle* or *People* probably wouldn't have been too enamored of Jesus' looks. Isaiah 53 declares that our savior "had no beauty or majesty to attract us to him, nothing in his appearance that we should desire him."

Though Jesus never urged folks to walk around with body odor and unwashed hair, he did admonish us to avoid being overly concerned with physical beauty, which fades with age in spite of tucks and Botox. What matters to God is inner beauty, which reveals itself in the practice of justice, mercy, and faith, and which is not only lifelong but eternal.

Ah, the glories of women's sports: the camaraderie. The quiet dignity. The proud refusal to buy into traditional stereotypes of beauty.
                                                    -- Sports Illustrated for Women

When it comes to looking good to God, it's what's inside that counts.

DAY 20

REST EASY

Read Hebrews 4:1-11.

*"There remains, then, a Sabbath rest for the people of God;
for anyone who enters God's rest also rests from his own
work, just as God did from his. Let us, therefore, make
every effort to enter that rest" (vv. 9-11).*

Bobby Bowden is a world-class napper.

Sportswriter Steve Ellis said Bowden is "notorious for his
catnaps, which can be taken at any time and any place." Defensive
coordinator Mickey Andrews recounted the time several coaches
were riding down an LA freeway on a recruiting trip. "We got a
bunch of coaches in there, and everybody is talking on their cell
phones setting up the next stop. There's all this buzz, and Coach
is sound asleep."

Former FSU coach Brad Scott recalled that on one recruiting
trip to Jacksonville, as the coaches left one house for another,
Bowden asked how far they had to go and was told five or ten
minutes. "OK, wake me up when we get there," he said. Scott said,
"I'm talking as soon as he said that, he'd be asleep. Almost snoring.
How he does it, I do not know. He'd wake up refreshed and ready
to go."

Immediately before the 1989 game against second-ranked
Miami, Bowden sought refuge from the craziness. He found
himself a chair in the locker room, leaned against a dry eraser
board, and promptly went to sleep. Time arrived for his pre-game

speech to the players, but still he napped. Finally, sports information director Rob Wilson yelled into Bowden's ear, "Five and a half minutes until kickoff." Bowden shook a little, jumped up, and gave his speech. Wilson insisted Bowden's nap affected the team, which was nervous until the players saw how relaxed their coach was. They calmed down and won 24-10.

Indispensable to physical health, rest for you may mean a good eight hours in the sack. Or a Saturday morning that begins in the backyard with the paper, a pot of coffee, and the soothing chorus of some dedicated and busy songbirds. Or a vacation in the mountains, where the most strenuous thing you do is change position in a hot tub.

God promised rest to you of a kind that is spiritual rather than physical, rest not for your weary body – which you can secure on your own -- but rest for your tortured and troubled soul.

God's rest comes through your faith: As you spend your day in the presence of God and in obedience to God's word for your life, you are revitalized and rejuvenated. Rest becomes a lifestyle, a way of coping with life's constant stress and pressure. The world around you may degenerate into chaos, but your soul remains at peace, nestled within the security of God's rest.

I can really see the value of napping now. If I don't do that, I'll be okay during practice, but as soon as I go home, wherever I am, I'm asleep.
— Bobby Bowden

God promises you spiritual rest that goes beyond
eight hours in the sack or a day spent lounging
in front of the TV set.

DAY 21

A HOLLYWOOD ENDING

Read Luke 24:1-12.

"Why do you look for the living among the dead? He is not here; he has risen!" (vv. 5, 6a)

It's the stuff of Hollywood. First black athlete to play football for a college. First game. And he makes the game-saving play. Twice. But it's not Hollywood fiction. It's the story of All-American and FSU Hall of Famer J.T. Thomas.

Thomas was one of four African-Americans on the FSU freshman football team in 1969 as the walls of desegregation were crumbling. In 1970, Thomas started at left corner, calling it "an awesome thing." But he understood the significance of what he was doing. "I was taking on the burden of being the first black football player at Florida State, and those were the headlines in the newspapers," he said.

The season opener was at home against Louisville, and FSU led 9-7 as the Cardinals lined up for a game-winning field goal in the closing seconds. Thomas blocked the kick "and everybody started cheering. We had the game won." But Thomas had been offsides and Louisville got another chance.

"I was down," Thomas said. "I thought I'd let down my team." When Thomas went into the huddle, though, Ron Wallace told him, "J.T., don't worry about it. You'll do it again." Thomas thought, "Block it again? Are you kidding me?" Apparently not, because the Noles lined up in the same formation and Thomas blocked the kick again. This time there were no flags.

"I couldn't have asked for a better ending to the game," Thomas said. It was such a Hollywood ending that a script writer couldn't dream it up – only it's true.

The world tells us that happy endings are for fairy tales and the movies, that reality is Cinderella dying in childbirth and her prince getting killed in a peasant uprising. But that's just another of the world's lies.

The truth is that Jesus Christ has been producing happy endings for almost two millennia. That's because in Jesus lies the power to change and to rescue a life no matter how desperate the situation. Jesus is the master at putting shattered lives back together, of healing broken hearts and broken relationships, of resurrecting lost dreams.

And as for living happily ever after, it's no fairy tale at all; God really means it. The greatest Hollywood ending of them all was written on a Sunday morning centuries ago when Jesus left a tomb and death behind. With faith in Jesus, your life can have that same ever-after ending. You live with God in peace, joy, and love – forever.

The End.

This field, this game, is a part of our past, Ray. It reminds us of all that once was good, and that could be again.
-- *James Earl Jones in* Field of Dreams

**Hollywood's happy endings are products
of imagination; the happy endings Jesus produces
are real and are yours for the asking.**

DAY 22

A SECOND CHANCE

Read John 7:53-8:11.

"'Then neither do I condemn you,' Jesus declared. 'Go now and leave your life of sin'" (v. 8:11).

Because of an incident with an iguana, Keith Kinderman's football playing days at FSU were over – until he got a second chance.

A Chicago native, Kinderman transferred to FSU as a junior before the 1961 season. He played in six games at running back/ cornerback and led the team with 393 yards rushing before he got kicked off the team.

What led to Kinderman's expulsion was a moment of gleeful inspiration that he proceeded unfortunately to turn into action. One evening as he was making the rounds of a few fraternity parties, Kinderman spotted an iguana in one of the frat houses. He promptly purloined the reptile, sneaked into a dorm, dropped the two-foot lizard into the middle of some sleepers, and flipped the light on. Some quite delightful havoc ensued, but once coach Bill Peterson heard about the practical joke, Kinderman was gone since this was his second offense.

Kinderman went back to Illinois and got a job in construction. "I thought my life was over," he said. Meanwhile, one of FSU's biggest boosters asked Peterson quite forcefully how he expected to win without Kinderman. Peterson had a school dean call Kinderman and inform him that though he was kicked off

SEMINOLES

the football team, he was still in school on a scholarship and he needed to get back to Tallahassee and get in class.

Kinderman didn't need any more convincing: "It was snowing, and I was working construction in about ten degrees. All I could envision was the good-looking Florida State honeys walking around campus with their short skirts." The next morning Kinderman and his 1953 Mercury hit the road for Tallahassee.

Given a second chance, Kinderman played both ways in 1962 and went on to play three years of pro ball.

"If I just had a second chance, I know I could make it work out." Ever said that? If only you could go back and tell your dad one last time you love him, take that job you passed up rather than relocate, or marry someone else. If only you had a second chance, a mulligan.

With God you always do. No matter how many mistakes you make, God will never give up on you. His mercy is limitless; nothing you can do puts you beyond his saving power. This means you always have a second chance because with God your future is not determined by your past or who you used to be. It is determined by your relationship with God through Jesus Christ.

God is ready and willing to give you a second chance – or a third chance or a fourth chance – if you will give him a chance.

I've seen people change their lives around, becoming entirely new human beings through faith.

– Bobby Bowden

**You get a second chance with God
if you give him a chance.**

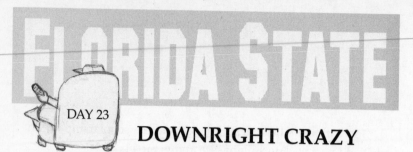

DAY 23

DOWNRIGHT CRAZY

Read Luke 13:31-35.

"Some Pharisees came to Jesus and said to him, 'Leave this place and go somewhere else. Herod wants to kill you.' He replied, 'Go tell that fox . . . I must keep going today and tomorrow and the next day'" (vv. 31-33).

In the quest for what would be described as "the biggest win in school history," FSU soccer coach Mark Krikorian did something that seemed downright crazy.

On Nov. 25, 2005, the Noles faced the second-ranked North Carolina Tar Heels in Chapel Hill. On the line was a berth in the College Cup, college soccer's equivalent of the Final Four. The Noles were 19-3-1 on the season, but history made them underdogs since they were 1-17 all-time against UNC, one of the sport's premier programs.

Regulation play and two overtimes decided nothing except how equally matched the two teams were. They wound up tied at one, and a best-of-five shootout would determine the berth in the Final Four. That's when Krikorian made his unorthodox and strange move.

Goalkeeper Ali Mims had been sensational all afternoon, fending off 31 Carolina shots during the 110 minutes of play. Backup Minna Pyykko had played only 106 minutes in goal all season. For the shootout, Krikorian decided to pull Mims for Pyykko. So how did it turn out? Pyykko stopped the second shot of a UNC All-America. That was the opening the Noles needed, and they prevailed 5-4 on the penalty kicks.

Why did Krikorian make such a move? His staff and he had consistently charted the goalkeepers' results against penalty kicks in practice. He also felt Pyykko would be more successful against the penalty kicks because Mims had lost some quickness and range on her dives after breaking her left leg in 2002.

Because of Krikorian's crazy but shrewd move, the Noles did indeed claim the biggest win in the soccer program's history.

What some see as crazy often is shrewd instead. Like the time you went into business for yourself or when you decided to go back to school. Maybe it was when you fixed up that old house. Or when you bought that new company's stock.

You know a good thing when you see it but are also shrewd enough to spot something that's downright crazy. Jesus was that way, too. He knew that entering Jerusalem was in complete defiance of all apparent reason and logic since a whole bunch of folks who wanted to kill him were waiting for him there.

Nevertheless, he went because he also knew that when the great drama had played out he would defeat not only his personal enemies but the most fearsome enemy of all: death itself.

It was, after all, a shrewd move that provided the way to your salvation.

Football is easy if you're crazy.

-- *Bo Jackson*

It's so good it sounds crazy -- but it's not: through faith in Jesus, you can have eternal life with God.

DAY 24

LIMITED-TIME OFFER

Read Psalm 103.

"As for man, his days are like grass, he flourishes like a flower of the field; the wind blows over it and it is gone. . . . But from everlasting to everlasting the Lord's love is with those who fear him" (vv. 15-17).

Eight-year-old Jesus Hernandez watched an entire boatload of men, women, and children drown.

After a year of prep school in Pennsylvania, Hernandez walked on at Florida State and earned a scholarship in 1992. He shared playing time at offensive tackle on the 1993 national championship team and went on to earn All-ACC honors as a senior in 1995. For Hernandez, it was a long, tough journey from walk-on to all-star to eventually signing a pro contract.

But he had made a difficult journey once before in his life, back when he was a child. In 1980, Hernandez and his mother, Idalia Sanabria, fled Cuba in a shrimp boat. Sanabria estimated that the decks of their boat were crammed with at least twice their usual capacity of two hundred people.

Jesus and she had originally been assigned to a smaller boat that had left two hours before Sanabria's did. A family of four behind them in line had included an ill, wheelchair-confined child, and the family had begged Sanabria for her two places on the boat so they could all travel together. "My mom gave up our spot for them," Hernandez said.

Sanabria's act of generosity saved both their lives. The crossing became perilous when a storm blew in. "Because our boat was bigger," she related, "we caught up to where we could see the little boat ahead of us. We saw it capsize and go into like a whirlpool. We saw them all die. We saw the sea swallow them."

A heart attack, cancer, or an accident such as that encountered during a storm at sea or on an interstate highway will probably take -- or has already taken -- someone you know or love who is "too young to die" such as that ill child on that boat.

The death of a younger person never seems to "make sense." That's because such a death belies the common view of death as the natural end of a life lived well and lived long. Moreover, you can't see the whole picture as God does, so you can't know how the death furthers God's kingdom.

At such a time, you can seize the comforting truth that God is in control and therefore everything will be all right one day. You can also gain a sense of urgency in your own life by appreciating that God's offer of life through Jesus Christ is a limited-time offer that expires at your death – and there's no guarantee about when that will be.

No one knows when he or she is going to die, so if we're going to accept Christ, we'd better not wait because death can come in the blink of an eye.

-- Bobby Bowden

**God offers you life through Jesus Christ,
but you must accept it before your death
because that's when the offer expires.**

DAY 25

DYNASTY

Read 2 Samuel 7:8-17.

"Your house and your kingdom will endure forever before me; your throne will be established forever" (v. 16).

It's called "the dynasty," and college football may well never see its like again.

The dynasty began in 1987 and ran for fourteen seasons, an incredible span during which Florida State's football team never finished out of the top five nationally. It's not just something FSU fans cooked up; the NCAA recognizes the Seminoles' run as one of the four "official" dynasties between 1981 and 2000.

During the unmatched stretch of greatness, FSU became the first (and still the only) school in major college football history to have ten or more wins in each of fourteen straight seasons. As a sideline to their dynasty, from the 1985 Gator Bowl through the Jan. 1, 1996, Orange Bowl, the Seminoles won eleven straight bowl games, an NCAA record.

The next-best record of any college program during that span belonged to the Miami Hurricanes; the Canes finished in the top five seven times. Then came Nebraska and Florida with five each, and Colorado, Michigan, and Notre Dame with four times each. During FSU's run, all of those other schools finished out of the top ten at least four times.

The Seminoles began play in the Atlantic Coast Conference in 1992 and won a record-setting nine straight conference titles during the run. FSU also won two national championships during the dynasty, in 1993 and 1999. They would certainly have won more except for losses to Miami on missed kicks. As Coach Bobby Bowden put it, "When I die, they'll chisel on my tombstone, 'But he played Miami.'" FSU lost only sixteen regular-season games during the streak; seven of those losses were to Miami, though the Noles did whip the Hurricanes five times in a row at one stretch.

Every dynasty – even Florida State's -- ends as events conspire to snap all winning streaks. Life in general and your life in particular is a matter of winning some and losing some. You seek to align yourself and be a part of a winning team in all areas of your life, but even then the definition of a winning team is not that it goes undefeated, but that it wins more than it loses.

Only one winning streak will never end; only one dynasty will never fall. It's God's own, for which the reigning king is Jesus. God promised David a kingdom that will never end and fulfilled that promise in David's descendant, Jesus.

It's done; the dynasty is established and the unstoppable, unending, eternal winning has begun. You can still lose, though; all you have to do is just stand on the sidelines and not get in the game.

Dynasties, streaks, and careers all come to an end eventually.
-- ESPN's Mr. Clean

All dynasties and win streaks end except the one
God established with Jesus as its king;
this one never loses and never will.

THE WORD

Read Matthew 12:33-37.

*"For out of the overflow of the heart the mouth speaks.
The good man brings good things out of the good stored
up in him, and the evil man brings evil things out of the
evil stored up in him" (vv. 34b-35).*

Corey Simon saw a team in trouble, so he did something. He
spoke up.

Simon was one of the most dominating defensive linemen in
FSU history. In 1999, his senior season, he was All-America and
All-ACC and tied Ron Simmons' team record with 44 tackles
for losses. He was the sixth pick in the 2000 NFL draft and was
a Pro-Bowl player. As the Noles prepared for Clemson in 1999,
though, Simon was not concerned at all about awards and a pro
career. What he wanted more than anything else was a national
title. What he saw was a team about to let it slip away.

Everything looked all right. The Noles were undefeated and
ranked No. 1. But Simon saw the team losing focus, losing sight of
its purpose, because of off-the-field distractions and turmoil.

So the senior leader who had a reputation as a quiet man acted.
He called the team together for a players-only meeting and led
the discussion.

Simon spoke straight from his heart. He told his teammates,
"Guys, we're not playing as a team. We're not playing as good as
we can." Junior linebacker Brian Allen said what Simon did was

"astonishing," showing "the magnitude of his leadership."

Simon wanted to be sure he could look back on his senior season and say that he did everything he could to help his team win a championship. So he shed his quiet demeanor and became the vocal leader the team needed.

Five games later, the Seminoles were undefeated national champions.

These days, everybody's got something to say and likely as not a place to say it. Talk radio, 24-hour sports and news TV channels, Talk has really become cheap.

But words still have power, and that includes not just those of the talking heads, hucksters, and pundits on television, but yours also. Your words are perhaps the most powerful force you possess for good or for bad. The words you speak today can belittle, wound, humiliate, and destroy. They can also inspire, heal, protect, and create. Your words both shape and define you. They also reveal to the world the depth of your faith.

Don't ever make the mistake of underestimating the power of the spoken word. After all, speaking the Word was the only means Jesus had to get his message across – and look what he managed to do.

Watch what you say because others sure will.

I have an obligation to set an example, not by saying, 'Do as I say, not as I do.' Coaches must set an example in . . . language.
– Bobby Bowden

**Choose your words carefully; they are the most
powerful force you have for good or for bad.**

DAY 27

DREAM WORLD

Read Joel 2:26-28.

"Your old men will dream dreams, your young men will see visions" (v. 28).

Bob Sura passed on immediate fame and fortune to pursue a dream.

On April 13, 1994, sweating under the glare of hot, bright television lights, Sura spoke at a press conference to make an announcement that was different from the norm: He disclosed that he was not going to the NBA and would instead return to FSU for his senior season.

It wasn't just the lights that made Sura sweat. It was also the thought of the world out there beyond college, the world of the NBA. He admitted it scared him, this world of "agents, plane trips, unfamiliar faces, few promises and no guarantees." He had thought about it long and hard, but in the end he finally decided he wasn't ready for life in the NBA.

Sura turned away from the money and the glitz and the glory in part also because there was something else out there he wanted to chase. Sura had a dream. He wanted to become FSU's all-time leading scorer. After his junior season, he was only 192 points shy of Jim Oler's 38-year-old record.

So he came back to make his dream come true. He finished his FSU career with 2,130 points, the only player in Seminole history to score more than 2,000 points. He was also the first player in

FSU history to be named first-team All-ACC. And the NBA? He was drafted in 1995 in the first round by the Cleveland Cavaliers.

Bob Sura stayed with his dream – and he got wealth and fame too.

You have dreams. Maybe to make a lot of money. Write the great American novel. Or have the fairy-tale romance.

But dreams all too often are crushed beneath the unavoidable and often oppressive weight of simple, everyday living; reality, not dreams, comes to occupy your time, your attention, and your effort. You have rather reluctantly come to understand that achieving your dreams requires a combination of persistence, timing, and providence.

But what if your dreams don't come true because they're not good enough? That is, they're based on the alluring but unreliable promises of the world rather than the true promises of God, which are a sure thing.

God calls us to great achievements because God's dreams for us are even greater than our dreams for ourselves. Such greatness occurs, though, only when our dreams and God's will for our lives are the same. Your dreams should be worthy of your best – and worthy of God's involvement in making them come true.

An athlete cannot run with money in his pocket. He must run with hope in his heart and dreams in his head.
-- Olympic Gold Medalist Emil Zatopek

Dreams based on the world's promises
are often crushed; those based on God's promises
are a sure thing.

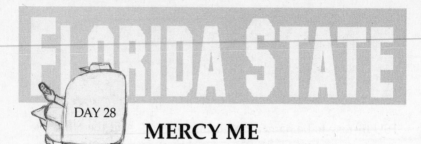

DAY 28

MERCY ME

Read Ephesians 2:1-10.

"Because of his great love for us, God, who is rich in mercy, made us alive with Christ even when we were dead in transgressions – it is by grace you have been saved" (vv. 4-5).

Somebody was trying to tell me Miami was too pitiful to hate. But that's just not true."

Seminole Boosters Executive Director Charlie Barnes spoke those words declaring there would be no mercy for the Miami Hurricanes before the 1997 game on Oct. 4. Miami was 1-3; fourth-ranked FSU was 3-0 and a 20-point favorite, but Seminole fans wanted to hear nothing about showing Miami any mercy. "Take it easy on the Canes?" one incredulous FSU fan said. "How does obliteration sound?" "I hope we overwhelm them and destroy their hopes and dreams," Barnes said.

The Seminole Nation probably will never get enough of whipping the team that caused them more heartache during the Bobby Bowden era than everybody else combined. Pity was in short supply for Miami, even though the Canes were a shadow of their former powerhouse selves, limping into Tallahassee depleted by injuries, suspensions, and a "crippling NCAA schol-arship-reduction penalty for various and sundry crimes against humanity and the NCAA rulebook."

Seminole fans remembered. "Those of us who were sitting in

SEMINOLES

the Orange Bowl in 1988, No-1 ranked in the nation and had to eat the short end of a 0-31 score will find today enjoyable and probably not filling enough, no matter what the final score is," Barnes said. But it might very well have been almost enough, even for Barnes. In the most lopsided FSU win in the history of the series, the Noles overwhelmed, destroyed, and buried the hapless, helpless Canes. They showed no mercy in a 47-0 whipping.

Somebody sometime in your life has hurt you. What's your attitude toward them? Do you scream for revenge and payback? Or do you extend mercy, showing compassion and kindness all out of proportion to what's been done to you?

Mercy is the appeal of last resort. When you are guilty – and Miami certainly was of spoiling some FSU seasons – and your sentence is sure – as Miami's was before the 1997 game -- your only hope is mercy. Your only prayer is that the judge will not remorselessly hand down the sentence you deserve.

Of all God's attributes, none is more astounding than his penchant for mercy. Through Jesus, God provided the way to save us from the sentence we deserve. Through Jesus, God made his divine mercy available to us all. In so doing, though, God expects that we who avail ourselves of his mercy will show mercy toward others. We reap what we sow.

If you race merely for the tributes from others, you will be at the mercy of their expectations.
-- Professional triathlete Scott Tinley

**To sow mercy in our lifetimes now
is to reap mercy from God
when we stand guiltily before him.**

DAY 29

GOD'S WORKFORCE

Matthew 9:35-38.

"Then he said to his disciples, 'The harvest is plentiful but the workers are few. Ask the Lord of the harvest, therefore, to send out workers into his harvest field'" (vv. 37-38).

JoAnne Graf retired in June 2008 as the winningest coach in college softball history, a Seminole institution to rival Bobby Bowden and Mike Martin in that the field on which her teams played was named after her. The basic attribute that powered her success was hard work.

When Graf first played for the Noles in 1973, the team played on the intramural fields, and men's intramurals frequently booted them over to the band field. No one had any scholarship money; the players packed their own lunches, car-pooled to games, and paid for meals and gas out of their own pockets.

Throughout her career, Graf addressed with university administrators the inequities between the men's and women's programs, and she often won because of her reputation for openness and honesty. By the time she retired, her softball team had the same travel accommodations as the baseball team, the maximum number of scholarships allowed by the NCAA, and a showpiece of a softball complex.

When Graf took the job of head coach in 1979, fast-pitch softball was five seasons away. Yet, she made the change from slow-pitch effortlessly (after winning two national championships), never

SEMINOLES

having a losing season and winning ten ACC championships. Her overall record was 1,437-478-6.

More than anything else, Graf was always a hard worker. Even after a day of planning and coaching, at home at night, she was "usually always thinking about stuff to do and what to do the next day."

JoAnne Graf worked her way to the top of her profession.

Do you embrace hard work or try to avoid it whenever it's even remotely possible? No matter how hard you may try, you really can't escape hard work. Funny thing about all these labor-saving devices like cell phones and laptop computers: You're working longer and harder than ever.

For many of us, our work defines us perhaps more than any other aspect of our lives. But there's a workforce you're a part of that doesn't show up in any Labor Department statistics or any IRS records.

You're part of God's staff; God has a specific job that only you can do for him. It's often referred to as a "calling," but it amounts to your serving God where there is a need in the way that best suits your God-given abilities and talents.

You should stand ready to work for God all the time, 24-7. Those are awful hours, but the benefits are out of this world.

I've always believed that if you put in the work, the results will come.
— Michael Jordan

God calls you to work for him using the talents and gifts he gave you; whether you're a worker or a malingerer is up to you.

DAY 30

CHANGE MASTER

Read Romans 6:1-14.

"Just as Christ was raised from the dead through the glory of the Father, we too may live a new life" (v. 4).

In 1992, Bobby Bowden demonstrated he wasn't too old to change.

The media recognize FSU's 1992 win over Georgia Tech as the official birth of the fast-break, no-huddle offense, but the Seminoles had tinkered with the revolutionary offense against Miami two games earlier. FSU had run a two-minute offense for some seasons, but the success of the offense run by Charlie Ward in a 19-16 loss to Miami convinced Bowden to "take it up a notch."

Two games later against Tech, "We're playing conventional offense and the game gets out of control," Bowden recalled. In fact, Tech led 21-7 early in the fourth quarter. Offensive coordinator Brad Scott said he and quarterbacks coach Mark Richt agreed that the no-huddle offense was their only chance to win the game. "And Coach Bowden said – 'Run the dadgum thing and see what happens.'"

What happened was that FSU rallied for a 29-24 win, and Bowden had confirmation of what he had suspected against Miami: "Boy, that Charlie was something out of that shotgun."

During the offseason, Scott and Richt visited the Buffalo Bills and the Tampa Bay Buccaneers to gain information on a blocking scheme to protect Ward. The offense then exploded full-scale in 1993 – and the result was a national championship.

Terry Bowden was impressed by his father's willingness to change: "Here my old man is 63 years old that year, and he's deciding if he can change and do something first before somebody else. . . . And it won him a national championship."

Anyone who asserts no change is needed in his or her life just isn't paying attention. Every life has doubt, worry, fear, failure, frustration, unfulfilled dreams, and unsuccessful relationships in some combination. The memory and consequences of our past often haunt and trouble us.

While it's an important and necessary beginning, simply recognizing the need for change in our lives doesn't mean the changes that will bring about hope, joy, peace, and fulfillment will occur. We need some power greater than ourselves or we wouldn't be where we are.

So where can we turn to? Where lies the hope for a changed life? It lies in an encounter with the one who is the Lord of all hope: Jesus Christ. For a life turned over to Jesus, change is inevitable. With Jesus in charge, the old self with its painful and destructive ways of thinking, feeling, loving, and living is transformed.

A changed life is always only a talk with Jesus away.

Dad is a great example of a guy who has never been afraid to make a change.

-- *Terry Bowden*

**In Jesus lie the hope and the power
that change lives.**

A JOYFUL NOISE

Read Psalm 100.

"Make a joyful noise to the Lord, all the earth" (v. 1 NRSV).

If it's game day in Tallahassee, it must be noisy, and the noisiest bunch of all dresses alike and sits together.

No less an expert than *Sports Illustrated* declared in December 1982 that "Florida State occasionally may lose a football game, but never a halftime show." That unique distinction of being forever undefeated belongs to the Marching Chiefs. With more than 460 members, FSU's college marching band is the largest in the world and one of the best.

The forerunner of today's band was organized in the 1930s with fewer than twenty female members. Everything changed with the arrival of male students in 1947, and that included the marching band. The student government association sponsored a newspaper survey to select a name for the band, and the Marching Chiefs made their first appearance at Stetson University in 1949.

Through the 1950s and '60s, the band grew and its traditions took shape. "The Hymn to the Garnet and the Gold" was played and sung for the first time after homecoming in 1958. The band grew to more than 200 members by 1971 when the Chiefs were finalists in ABC's Best College Marching Band Contest. In 1991 the Chiefs – now more than 400 strong – became the first college band to produce its own CD.

The Marching Chiefs have been world travelers over the years, but it is on the field and in the stands of Doak S. Campbell Stadium that they are most at home – and the noisiest as they set the place to rockin' and rollin' as only they can.

Maybe you can't play a lick or carry a tune in the proverbial bucket. Or perhaps you do know your way around a guitar or a keyboard and can sing "The Hymn to the Garnet and the Gold" on karaoke night without closing the joint down.

Unless you're a professional musician, though, how well you play or sing really doesn't matter except to your own ego and to your outlandish fantasies about being a rock star. What counts is that you have music in your heart and sometimes you have to turn it loose – especially when the Noles score and the Marching Chiefs play.

That same boisterous and noisy enthusiasm should also be a part of the joy you have in your worship of God. Making "a joyful noise" to the Lord means just that, busting forth with a racket for God.

When you consider that God loves you and always will, how can you help but shout, holler, and sing – or even whisper -- your love in return?

I would like to think I'd probably gone into the military. And I like music. I might have liked to have been a bandleader.

-- *Bobby Bowden*

You call it music; others may call it noise.
If it's joyful, send some God's way.

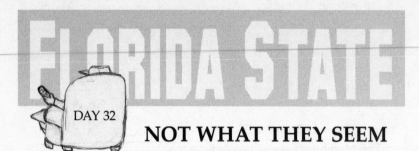

NOT WHAT THEY SEEM

Read Habakkuk 1:2-11.

"Why do you make me look at injustice? Why do you tolerate wrong? Destruction and violence are before me; there is strife, and conflict abounds" (v. 3).

The Seminoles doused Coach Bobby Bowden with Gatorade and rushed onto the field to celebrate their national championship. Only they weren't champions yet because even though the clock had expired, the game wasn't over.

FSU met Nebraska for the national title in the 1994 Orange Bowl. Freshman Scott Bentley kicked a 22-yard field goal with only 21 seconds left to give the Seminoles an 18-16 lead. A good kickoff return and an unsportsmanlike conduct penalty gave the Cornhuskers life at their own 43. A second-down pass was complete to the FSU 28, but the last of those interminable 21 seconds ticked off the clock and the celebration began.

Bowden trotted onto the field and shook hands with Cornhusker head coach Tom Osborne, both of them convinced the game was over. Jubilant Florida State players and fans gathered around to enjoy winning the ultimate prize in college football. But things were not what they seemed. To the dismay of FSU supporters everywhere, one of the game officials declared that one second was left on the clock. Nebraska had time for a game-winning field goal.

Bowden's immediate concern was where the ball would be

spotted. The refs said the 33-yard-line, and Bowden knew the Nebraska kicker's maximum range was 47 yards. "So I'm thinking, 'No sweat,'" Bowden said. But then an official told Bowden, "Coach, we were wrong. We got to move the ball up five more yards." Now Bowden thought, "Can you believe this? Not only did they get one second back, but they got five yards out of it."

The 45-yard attempt was wide left, and this time FSU had won the national championship.

Sometimes in life things are just not what they seem. Like nothing before it, the attack on the World Trade Center forced us to confront the possibility of a new reality: that we are helpless in the face of anarchy; that injustice, destruction, and violence are pandemic in and symptomatic of our modern age. It seems that anarchy is winning, that the system of standards, values, and institutions we have cherished is crumbling while we watch.

But we should not be deceived or disheartened. God is in fact the arch-enemy of chaos, the creator of order and goodness and the architect of all of history. God is in control. We often misinterpret history as the record of mankind's accomplishments -- which it isn't -- rather than the unfolding of God's plan -- which it is. That plan has a clearly defined end: God will make everything right. In that day things will be what they seem.

We won twice.
-- Bobby Bowden on the win over Nebraska

The forces of good and decency often seem
helpless before evil's power, but don't be fooled;
God is in control and will set things right.

DAY 33

CLOTHES HORSE

Read Genesis 37:1-11.

*"Israel loved Joseph more than all his children, because
he was the son of his old age: and he made him a coat of
many colours" (v. 3 KJV).*

In Fred Biletnikoff's case, clothes did not make the man.

Biletnikoff is FSU's first consensus All-America (1964) and a
member of both the college and the pro football halls of fame. Each
year the Fred Biletnikoff Award is presented by the Tallahassee
Quarterback Club Foundation to the nation's most outstanding
college receiver. He was such a campus hero that once when he
was injured, students gathered outside his dorm and sang "Get
Well, Freddie" to the tune of "Hello, Dolly."

But as one writer said, "Fred Biletnikoff cut neither an
imposing nor a dashing figure." Al Davis of the Oakland Raiders,
who presented Biletnikoff for induction into the Pro Football Hall
of Fame, said, "Genius comes in many different configurations."
Biletnikoff's uniform was never stylish. He wore loose sleeves
and baggy socks, hand cut his uniform to his liking, blackened
his eyes, and saturated his hands and his uniforms with a gooey
substance he called "stickum."

Disdaining fashionable footwear, long after Ridell quit making
a particular style of shoe, Biletnikoff located and furnished the
company with kangaroo leather so they could make him the
old shoe. He refused to switch to the newer and more protective

helmets and changed over to the two-bar facemask only after he suffered a number of broken noses.

Sportswriter Gary Long said, "The thinning, dirty-blond hair that hung damply and limply down to his neck when Biletnikoff would take off his helmet added an exclamation point to his raggedy appearance."

Fred Biletnikoff was no fashion plate; he was just great.

Contemporary society proclaims that it's all about the clothes. Buy that new suit or dress, those new shoes, and all the sparkling accessories, and you'll be a new person. The changes are only cosmetic, though; under those clothes, you're the same person. Consider Joseph, for instance, prancing about in his pretty new clothes; he was still a spoiled tattletale.

Jesus never taught that we should run around half-naked or wear only second-hand clothes from the local mission. He did warn us, though, against making consumer items such as clothes a priority in our lives.

A follower of Christ seeks to emulate Jesus not through material, superficial means such as wearing special clothing like a robe and sandals. Rather, the disciple desires to match Jesus' inner beauty and serenity -- whether the clothes the Christian wears are the sables of a king or the rags of a pauper.

You can't call golf a sport. You don't run, jump, you don't shoot, you don't pass. All you have to do is buy some clothes that don't match.
-- Former major leaguer Steve Sax

**Where Jesus is concerned, clothes don't make
the person; faith does.**

MYSTERIOUS WAYS

Read Romans 11:25-36.

"O the depth of the riches and wisdom and knowledge of God! How unsearchable are his judgments and how inscrutable his ways!" (v. 33 NRSV)

The good Lord sure works in mysterious ways." That old statement of faith certainly applies to the life of FSU women's basketball player Tamara Gracey.

Little went right in Gracey's young life for a while. Her mother became ill, and she had to transfer from Kansas to Tulsa to take care of her. When she had to put her mother in a nursing home, she had to drop out of school entirely to pay the bills. She was out of school for two years, but she never gave up hope or her faith. And because of the latter, God stepped in.

In Marshall, Ind., in the summer of 1997, Gracey shared her faith and her story with students at a Fellowship of Christian Athletes camp. She told them, "I've really been praying about an opportunity to go back to school, get an education, and really be able to take care of my mom like I want to."

In the audience, on her first day on the job as head coach of the Florida State women's basketball team, was Sue Semrau. When Gracey spoke, she looked down at the aisle to assistant coach Theresa Gernatt and asked, "Do we have a scholarship?" Gernatt said they had one. Gracey, a 6-foot forward, became the one.

After sitting out a year, Gracey played in all 27 games in 1998-99 as a senior. Her free-throw percentage for that season ranks in the top ten all time. "This is where God wanted me to be," she said. "It just seems like things just happen out of the blue."

We often love a good mystery because we relish the challenge of uncovering what somebody else wants to hide. We are intrigued by a perplexing whodunit, a rousing round of Clue, or Perry Mason reruns.

As Tamara Gracey's life illustrates, some mysteries are simply beyond our knowing. Those things "out of the blue" that are in actuality the mysterious ways of God remain so to us because we can't see the divine machinations. We can see only the results, appreciate that God was behind it all, and give him thanks and praise.

Ultimately, God has revealed a great deal about himself, especially through Jesus, but much about the divine master and creator of the universe still remains unknowable. Why, for instance, does he tolerate the existence of evil? Just exactly how did he hang those stars up there? What does he really look like? Why is he so obviously fond of bugs? Those and many more questions remain.

We know for sure, though, that God is love, and so we proceed with life, assured that one day all mysteries will be revealed.

Through sports, a coach can offer a boy a way to sneak up on the mystery of manhood.
— Writer Pat Conroy

God chooses to keep much about himself
shrouded in mystery, but one day
we will see and understand.

STAR POWER

Read Luke 10:1-3, 17-20.

"The Lord appointed seventy-two others and sent them two by two ahead of him to every town and place where he was about to go" (v. 1).

Two Heisman Trophy winners and a slew of All-Americas notwithstanding, one of the most famous of all former FSU football players is Lee Corso.

Corso, of course, became a star for his 20-plus years of serving as a college football analyst for ESPN. In 1953, though, he was "arguably the most consequential recruit in FSU's neophyte football history." Corso was all-state in three sports in high school and was recruited vigorously by Miami, Clemson, Florida, and a host of others.

Seminole head coach Tom Nugent persuaded him to come to Tallahassee by promising him he could play baseball and football. Corso said he chose FSU because "I could come in with the 1953 recruiting class and help build something at Florida State, as compared to maintaining programs at schools such as Clemson."

Before he left FSU, quarterback/halfback/tailback Corso had led the team in kick returns in 1954, in rushing in 1955, and in passing in 1956 and had set a school record with 14 career interceptions. Before his sophomore season, the coaches moved him to tailback where he played ahead of another FSU football player who became a national star: Burt Reynolds. "Reynolds was one of the toughest kids we ever had on our team," Corso said. "He was rough, strong, and was a really aggressive runner."

Corso had a tough side himself. He played half the 1955 baseball season on an ankle that had been broken in the Sun Bowl and misdiagnosed as a sprain. Corso was elected into the FSU Sports Hall of Fame in 1978.

Football teams are like other organizations in that they may have a star but the star would be nothing without the supporting cast. It's the same in a private company, in a government bureaucracy, in a military unit, and just about any other team of people with a common goal.

That includes the team known as a church. It may have its "star" in the preacher, who is – like the quarterback or the company CEO – the most visible representative of the team. Preachers are, after all, God's paid, trained professionals.

But when Jesus assembled a team of seventy-two folks, he didn't have anybody on the payroll or any seminary graduates. All he had were no-names who loved him. And nothing has changed. God's church still depends on those whose only pay is the satisfaction of serving and whose only qualification is their love for God. God's church needs you.

You may have the greatest bunch of individual stars in the world, but if they don't play together, the club won't be worth a dime.
— Babe Ruth

Yes, the church needs its professional clergy,
but it also needs those who serve as volunteers
because they love God; the church needs you.

DAY 36

CLOCKWORK

Read Matthew 25:1-13.

"Keep watch, because you do not know the day or the hour" (v. 13).

Bobby Bowden hated so badly to waste time that an assistant coach once worried about being fired after he talked Bowden into taking a recruiting trip that was a bust.

Widely known for his recruiting savvy as well as his coaching ability, Bowden nevertheless despised making trips that he wasn't convinced would yield results. He often argued, "A phone call saves money and time." Assistant coach Jim Gladden said Bowden would "do anything if he feels you can get the guy. But if it's a wild goose chase—"

Wally Burnham once took Bowden on such a chase all the way to Fort Myers. "I got Coach to go down there and visit [the recruit] on a Saturday," Burnham recalled. He had it all planned out. They would "get down to Fort Myers at 8:00 a.m., have breakfast with [the recruit] and his mom, and get back to Tallahassee in time for everything to get started for the recruiting weekend."

So Burnham and Bowden flew down on a state plane and made it to the recruit's front door according to schedule. But then Burnham saw a piece of paper taped to the door. With a sinking feeling, he read, "Coach, sorry we could not be here. We had to go shopping." The recruit's mother signed the note.

They had been stood up!

SEMINOLES

"I thought I was going to be fired," a fretful Burnham said. "That's the most scared I've ever been." It got worse: The recruit signed with Notre Dame. Bowden's trip was a complete waste of time.

We may pride ourselves on our time management, but we only fool ourselves. The truth is that we don't manage time; it manages us. Hurried and harried, we live by schedules that seem to have too much what and too little when. By setting the bedside alarm at night, we even let the clock determine how much down time we get.

A life of leisure actually means living in such a manner that time is of no importance. That doesn't include vacations; more than likely when we're on that trip of a lifetime, we're fretting about how much work is piling up in our absence.

Every second of our life – all the time we have – is a gift from God, who dreamed up time in the first place. We would do well, therefore, to ponder what God considers to be good time management and to remember that Jesus himself warned us against mismanaging the time we have.

From God's point of view, using our time wisely means being prepared at every moment for Jesus' return, which will occur -- well, only time will tell when.

We didn't lose the game; we just ran out of time.

– Vince Lombardi

We mismanage our time when we fail to prepare for Jesus' return even though we don't know when that will be.

DAY 37

THE GOOD OLD DAYS

Read Psalm 102.

"My days vanish like smoke; . . . but you remain the same, and your years will never end" (vv. 3, 27).

Everyone sometimes yearns to return to a time in the past we have come to regard as the good old days. The exception may well be FSU football.

Hugh Adams was a tackle/center at FSU in 1948 and '49. Adams' dorm was an Air Force barracks at Dale Mabry Field. He practiced football and dined on the base. Adams described the accommodations as "spartan but quite satisfactory." He was used to them, having served in World War II.

The team traveled to road games in an old school bus. The competition was a little different, too. The 1949 team, for instance, opened the season against Whiting Field, a team from a military base, and won 74-0.

Buddy Strauss was another Seminole back there in the good old days, playing fullback and defensive back in 1948-49. Since he was from Tallahassee, he avoided the barracks by living at home.

When FSU went to Selma in 1949 to play Livingston State, they arrived to find that the Livingston coaches had forgotten to hire any officials for the game. The coaches went into the stands and talked some former players into officiating the game. As Strauss put it, "It was pretty tough getting a call." Livingston won 13-6.

The Noles bounced back to finish 8-1 and beat Tampa for the

championship of the Dixie Conference, which earned the team a berth in the Cigar Bowl in Tampa. Adams said, "It was a big deal for us, but I can't say how big it was for other people." FSU beat Wofford 19-6 for its first-ever bowl win back there in those "good old days" that in reality weren't nearly as good as what FSU fans have come to enjoy these days.

It's a brutal truth that time just never stands still. The current of your life sweeps you along until you realize one day you've lived long enough to have a past. Part of it you cling to fondly. The stunts you pulled with your high-school buddies. Your first apartment. That dance with your first love. That special vacation. Those "good old days."

You hold on relentlessly to the memory of those old, familiar ways because of the stability they provide in an uncertain world. The precious recollections of a time you can never recapture will always be there even as times change and you age.

Another constant exists in your life, too. God has been a part of every event in your life that created a memory because he was there. He's always there with you; the question is whether you ignore him or make him a part of your day.

A "good old day" is any day shared with God.

Years ago, you used to get out and fight and run around and chase each other with a jackhammer and stuff like that. Those were the good old days.

-- *Dale Earnhardt, Jr. on NASCAR track etiquette*

Today is one of the "good old days"
if you share it with God.

THE UNEXPECTED

Read Luke 2:1-20.

"She gave birth to her firstborn, a son. She wrapped him in cloths and placed him in a manger, because there was no room for them in the inn" (v. 7).

About the only thing more unexpected than FSU's win over Duke in 1993 was the player who nailed the winning shot.

The Seminoles surprised the two-time defending national champions and sixth-ranked Blue Devils 89-88 in an overtime thriller, which was regarded as an upset since the Seminoles were 12-5 but weren't ranked. This FSU team was pretty good, though, with a lineup featuring Bob Sura, Charlie Ward, Sam Cassell, and Doug Edwards. They finished the season 25-10 and advanced to the Elite Eight in the NCAA tournament before losing.

On Jan. 24, senior Byron Wells was the improbable hero as he "forever cemented his place in FSU basketball history." He came into the game averaging 5.1 points per game and barely played in the first half. But with a minute left in regulation, Edwards fouled out. That sent Wells into the game.

In overtime, Duke scored to lead 88-86 with only 15 seconds left. During a time out, Coach Pat Kennedy incredibly designed a play for Wells. But it wasn't such a strange idea. Cassell called Wells "the best stand-still shooter on the team."

Cassell drove inside and kicked the ball out to Wells. He had one foot on the three-point line, and "in what looked like a cocky move for a reserve forward," he stepped backward and let fly. "What's six inches?" he said. "You might as well take a step back and make sure it's a three." Wells hit the three, and FSU had an unexpected 89-88 win and an unexpected hero.

Just like the Duke Blue Devils, we think we've got everything figured out and planned for, and then something unexpected like Byron Wells happens. Someone gets ill; you fall in love; you lose your job; you're going to have another child; your car up and dies. Life surprises us with its bizarre and unexpected twists and turns.

God is that way also, catching us unawares to remind us he's still around and still in our lives. A friend who hears you're down and stops by to pray for you, a child's laugh, a bird's earnest song -- unexpected moments of love and beauty. God is like that, always doing something in our lives we didn't expect.

But why shouldn't he? There is absolutely nothing God can't do. The only factor limiting what God can do is the paucity of our own faith.

Expect the unexpected from God, this same deity who unexpectedly came to live among us as a man. He does, by the way, expect a response from you.

I had a good alibi ready. Then those crazy guys go out and win the game.

— Bobby Bowden on a last-minute win

God does the unexpected -- like showing up as Jesus -- to remind you of his presence, and now he expects a response from you.

DAY 39

HEAD GAMES

Read Job 28.

"The fear of the Lord – that is wisdom, and to shun evil is understanding" (v. 28).

The Seminoles had a chip-shot field goal that would give them the lead with about five minutes to play – and then Bobby Bowden started thinking.

In the 1982 game against Southern Mississippi, the Noles were tied at 17 when quarterback Kelly Lowrey led FSU on a late drive that stalled at the Golden Eagle two-yard line. All FSU had to do was convert what amounted to an extra point for a 20-17 lead that very well might hold up for the win.

But Bowden was thinking past the sure-shot field goal. "If they get the ball back, they'll drive down and get a field goal," Bowden told offensive coordinator George Henshaw. "We ain't stopping them. We can slow them down, but we have hardly been able to stop their guys, and they have plenty of time."

So he was actually considering a fake. Adding to the discussion was that after watching some Southern Miss films, Henshaw had drawn up and practiced a fake field goal he believed would work.

Bowden thought it through and made the call: "Let's do it. Let's go for it," he said, reasoning that Southern Miss would be convinced the Seminoles would kick "because three points win the game." In to hold for the kick, Lowrey took the snap, straightened up, and scored standing up.

Sure enough, Southern Miss stormed back down the field to the FSU 25 where the Eagles could have kicked a field goal to tie. But because Bowden had done some serious thinking, they didn't have the chance. The 24-17 score stood up.

You're a thinking person. When you talk about using your head, you're speaking as Bobby Bowden illustrated in that game against Southern Miss: Logic and reason are part of your psyche. A coach's bad call frustrates you, your boss's often inexplicable decisions bewilder you, and your children's frequent inexplicable behavior flummoxes you. Why can't people just think things through and act accordingly?

That goes for matters of faith, too. Jesus doesn't tell you to turn your brain off when you walk into a church or open the Bible. In fact, when you seek Jesus, you seek him heart, soul, body, and mind. The mind of the master should be the master of your mind so that you consider every situation in your life through the critical lens of the mind of Christ. With your head and your heart, you encounter God, who is, after all, the true source of wisdom.

To know Jesus is not to stop thinking; it is to start thinking divinely.

Football is more mental than physical, no matter how it looks from the stands.
-- Pro Hall-of-Fame linebacker Ray Nitschke

Since God is the source of all wisdom,
it's only logical that you encounter him
with your mind as well as your emotions.

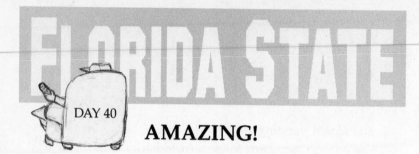

DAY 40

AMAZING!

Read: Luke 4:31-36.

"All the people were amazed and said to each other, 'What is this teaching? With authority and power he gives orders to evil spirits and they come out!'" (v. 36)

In the season opener of 1993's national championship year, the Noles turned in what may be the most amazing goal-line stand in college football history.

On Aug. 28, FSU trounced the Kansas Jayhawks 42-0 on the hot artificial turf of Giants Stadium. The hottest part of the day, though, was the FSU defense that amazing as it sounds, put together a 12-play goal-line stand.

Trailing 14-0 in the second quarter, the Jayhawks reached the FSU nine. Three times FSU apparently stopped the threat, but three times the Noles were called for offsides because Derrick Alexander's helmet was across the line. As the series unwound, Kansas had six cracks from the FSU one.

"I could hear Derrick [Brooks] behind me yelling, 'One more down, one more,'" linebacker Ken Alexander said. "The only problem was, it kept being one more down."

Finally, on the twelfth play, Ken Alexander ended the Kansas offense's misery by slamming into the shoulder pads of the Jayhawk back after Brooks had grabbed a foot and held on. The back's helmet crossed the goal line, but the ball didn't break the plane. This time there was no offsides call.

"It was probably the best goal-line stand I have seen," Coach Bobby Bowden said. Kansas head coach Glen Mason had another word for it: "That was embarrassing. Simply embarrassing."

Following that amazing goal-line stand, Charlie Ward led the offense on a 99-yard scoring drive that made it 21-0 at halftime and took the final bit of heart out of the Jayhawks.

The word *amazing* defines the limits of what you believe to be plausible. The Grand Canyon, the birth of your children, those last-second Seminole wins and bone-crunching defensive plays -- they're amazing! You've never seen anything like that before!

Some people in Galilee felt the same way when they first encountered Jesus. Jesus amazed them with the authority of his teaching, and he wowed them with his power over spirit beings. People everywhere just couldn't quit talking about him.

It would have been amazing had they not been amazed. They were, after all, witnesses to the most amazing spectacle in the history of the world: God himself was right there among them walking, talking, teaching, preaching, and healing.

Amazement to match theirs should be a part of your life too, because Jesus still lives. The almighty God of the universe seeks to spend time with you every day – because he loves you. Amazing!

It's amazing. Some of the greatest characteristics of being a winning football player are the same ones it's true of being a Christian man.

-- *Bobby Bowden*

**Everything about God is amazing,
but perhaps most amazing of all is
that he loves us and desires our company.**

CHEERS

Read Matthew 21:1-11.

"The crowds that went ahead of him and those that followed shouted" (v. 9).

It may well be the longest cheer in FSU sports history, and before it was completed, its object was a nervous wreck.

Statistically, the outbreak of cheering occurred during the most insignificant at-bat of Doug Mientkiewicz's day. Mientkiewicz is one of FSU's legendary baseball players with a career that includes a gold medal from the 2000 Olympics and a .306 average for the Minnesota Twins in 2001. He turned pro after his junior year in 1995, and it was during his last at-bat in Tallahassee that the home crowd showed its appreciation.

The occasion was the Atlantic Region I championship game against Mississippi on May 28. The Seminoles were on their way to the College World Series with a 13-1 lead, and Mientkiewicz was a big part of that. He had slammed a double and two home runs and driven in five runs. So absolutely nothing was on the line except ending his career on a high note when Mientkiewicz stepped into the batter's box for the last time.

That's when it started: "Give me an 'M.' Give me an 'I'." The crowd managed to spell out all twelve letters of his last name and even got it right. That task completed, the expected question, "What's that spell?" followed. Then came the thunderous and original answer of "Doug!"

SEMINOLES

By that time, a somewhat distracted Mientkiewicz found himself behind in the count one ball and two strikes. "All I was thinking was 'Don't strike out. Don't strike out,'" he said.

He didn't. He battled his way to a walk on this final trip to the plate as a Seminole when the crowd that included his mom and dad had given him something to remember forever with their cheers.

Chances are you go to work every day, do your job well, and then go home to your family. This country couldn't run without you; you're indispensable to the nation's efficiency. Even so, nobody cheers for you or waves pompoms in your face. Your name probably will never elicit a standing ovation if a PA announcer calls it.

It's just as well, since public opinion is notoriously fickle. Consider what happened to Jesus. When he entered Jerusalem, he was the object of raucous cheering and an impromptu parade. The crowd's adulation reached such a frenzy they tore branches off trees and threw their clothes on the ground.

Five days later the crowd shouted again, only this time they screamed for Jesus' execution.

So don't worry too much about not having your personal set of cheering fans. Remember that you do have one personal cheerleader who will never stop pulling for you: God.

A cheerleader is a dreamer that never gives up.

– Source unknown

**Just like the sports stars, you have
a personal cheerleader: God.**

DAY 42

THE SUB

Read Galatians 3:10-14.

*"Christ redeemed us from the curse of the law
by becoming a curse for us" (v. 13).*

Among the most exciting games in FSU football history was
the 1983 game against Arizona State when a substitute quarterback led the Noles to a last-second win.

FSU held grimly onto a 14-13 lead early in the fourth quarter
when starting quarterback Kelly Lowrey suffered a knee injury.
The Seminoles had to turn to Bob Davis, who had attempted
only eleven passes in his collegiate career. He also was suffering
a rather unique handicap: He played with only one contact lens,
having washed the other down his hotel sink.

The assistants urged Bobby Bowden, who was calling the
plays, to give Davis something easy to get him started. "Throw
something he can complete to give him confidence," they told
him.

Bowden apparently had a quite different notion about the way
to go about giving his substitute quarterback some confidence.
On Davis' fourth play, the coach called for a bomb. Davis hit it for
a 40-yard touchdown.

Despite Davis' early success, Arizona State led 26-22 with less
than two minutes to play. FSU had the ball on its own 18. What
followed is a legendary part of FSU lore known as "The Drive."
On fourth and five from the 23, Davis hit tight end Tim Wheeler

for a 16-yard gain to keep the Seminoles alive. Two plays later, Davis found Wheeler again, and he rambled all the way to the Sun Devil ten-yard line.

Then with only six seconds left, Davis, the incredible substitute, hit Jessie Hester in the end zone for the game winner. FSU won 29-26. "A great spectator game," Bowden said of the contest, which over the years always remained one of his favorites.

Wouldn't it be cool if you had a substitute like Bob Davis for all life's hard stuff? Telling of a death in the family? Call in your sub. Breaking up with your boyfriend? Job interview? Chemistry test? Crucial presentation at work? Let the sub handle it.

We do have such a substitute, but not for the matters of life. Instead, Jesus is our substitute for matters of life and death. Since Jesus has already made it, we don't have to make the sacrifice God demands for forgiveness and salvation.

One of the ironies of our age is that many people desperately grope for a substitute for Jesus. Mysticicm, human philosophies such as Scientology, false religions such as Hinduism and Islam, cults, New Age approaches that preach happiness without any responsibility or accountability – they and others like them are all pitiful, inadequate substitutes for Jesus.

Accept no substitutes. It's Jesus or nothing.

I never substitute just to substitute. The only way a guy gets off the floor is if he dies.

– Former basketball coach Abe Lemons

**There is no substitute for Jesus,
the consummate substitute.**

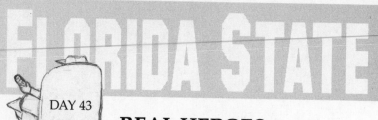

REAL HEROES

Read 1 Samuel 16:1-13.

*"Do not consider his appearance or his height, for . . .
the Lord does not look at the things man looks at. . . .
The Lord looks at the heart" (v. 7).*

Peter Boulware and Andre Wadsworth are two of the greatest defensive linemen in FSU football history, true Saturday heroes. On at least one occasion they acted heroically off the field to save an injured student's life.

As a junior in 1996, Boulware set a school record with 19 sacks. He was All-ACC and All-America and was named the National Defensive Player of the Year by *Football News*. Wadsworth finished his career at FSU in 1997 and was both All-ACC and All-America.

On the night of Nov. 25, 1996, though, they were just a couple of pals riding home after having seen the latest *Star Trek* movie. On Mission Road, Wadsworth, who was driving, suddenly said, "Hey, did you see that?" Reflecting on the movie, Boulware hadn't seen anything, but Wadsworth was convinced he had seen something strange in a truck on the side of the road.

He turned around, and they found the truck against a tree with a young man inside, who they would later learn was an FSU student. "His whole face was covered with blood," Boulware said. Wadsworth hurried back to his car and used his phone to call 911 while Boulware whipped off his Nike warm-up jacket and wrapped it around the injured man's head. They stayed with him, talking to him and keeping him conscious until an ambulance arrived.

Sgt. Ken Bergstrom of the Tallahassee Police Department described the duo's actions as heroic. "I don't think it was heroic," Boulware countered. "That's just the Lord working and just watching out for that guy."

A hero is commonly thought of as someone who performs brave and dangerous feats that save or protect someone's life – just as Andre Wadsworth and Peter Boulware did. You figure that excludes you.

But ask your son about that when you show him how to bait a hook, or your daughter when you show up for her dance recital. Look into the eyes of those Little Leaguers you help coach.

Ask God about heroism when you're steady in your faith. For God, a hero is a person with the heart of a servant. And if a hero is a servant who acts to save other's lives, then the greatest hero of all is Jesus Christ.

God seeks heroes today, those who will proclaim the name of their hero – Jesus – proudly and boldly, no matter how others may scoff or ridicule. God knows a hero when he sees him -- by what's in his heart.

Heroes and cowards feel exactly the same fear; heroes just act differently.
-- Boxing trainer Cus D'Amato

God's heroes are those who remain steady
in their faith while serving others.

DAY 44

SOUTHERN HOSPITALITY

Read 2 Kings 4:8-17.

"Let's make a small room on the roof and put in it a bed and a table, a chair and a lamp for him. Then he can stay there whenever he comes to us" (v. 10).

You would think the Seminoles might show a little Southern hospitality when they officially welcomed their Yankee brethren from Beantown into the Atlantic Coast Conference. Yeah, right.

The transformation of the ACC from a basketball conference to a conference that had the nation's greatest college basketball and football to match anybody else's was completed in 2005 when Boston College became the ACC's twelfth member. Miami and Virginia Tech had moved over from the Big East in 2004.

For its first-ever ACC football game on Sept. 17, Boston College drew Florida State. From the outset, the 2-0 Seminoles showed no inclination to be hospitable to the new kids on the block, doing the Southern two-step right into BC's Alumni Stadium and taking a 14-0 lead in the first 5:44 of the game.

Senior linebacker A.J. Nicholson intercepted BC's first-ever ACC pass and returned it 19 yards for a touchdown. For some reason, the Eagles threw in Nicholson's direction again, and he promptly stole another pass, setting up a 20-yard touchdown pass from Drew Weatherford to wideout Greg Carr.

But Boston College had been proffered the invitation to join the ACC largely because of the quality of its football program, so the Eagles weren't about to quit. They rallied and took a 17-14 lead at halftime. In the third quarter, though, Weatherford began picking BC apart. He hit eight-of-nine passes on a 10-play drive that ended with a five-yard TD pass to Carr. FSU never trailed again and won 28-17, displaying not even the slightest hint of Southern hospitality.

Southerners are deservedly famous for their hospitality. Down South, warmth and genuineness seem genetic. You open your home to the neighborhood kids, to your friends, to the stranger whose car broke down in the rain, to the stray cat that showed up hungry and hollering. You even let family members overstay their welcome without grumbling -- at least not to them.

Hospitality was vitally important to the cultures of Biblical times also. Travelers in those days faced innumerable dangers: everything from lions to bandits to deadly desert heat. Finding a temporary haven thus often became quite literally a matter of life and death.

Since hospitality is a sign of a loving and generous nature, it is not surprising that almighty God himself is a gracious host. He welcomes you, not as a stranger, but as an adopted child. One glorious day this hospitable God will open the doors of his place for you -- and never ask you to leave.

Being raised in the South means growing up on a diet of Southern hospitality and a dose of football every weekend.
— Askman.com

Hospitality is an outward sign of the inward loving and generous nature of the host.

DAY 45

OUT WITH THE OLD

Read Hebrews 8:3-13.

"The ministry Jesus has received is as superior to theirs as the covenant of which he is mediator is superior to the old one, and it is founded on better promises" (v. 6).

The old days of women's athletics at FSU have been superseded by the new age, and nobody's looking back.

Once upon a time, the women's teams at FSU had no budgets, no scholarships, and no facilities. The first Seminole women's intercollegiate team – volleyball – was fielded in 1968. Until then, athletic competition for women consisted of intramurals and so-called "sports days."

Graduate students and professors were the first coaches, unpaid volunteers who coached after a full day in the classroom. Marlene Furnell was a graduate student when she was named FSU's first women's athletics director in 1973. The first full-time paid women's coaches came in 1976.

Practices were held at night after the men's teams – or the marching band – had abandoned the courts or fields. Coaches had to raise money for uniforms and equipment. Teams often traveled by station wagons, sleeping four to a motel room or staying at parents' homes. When the Seminole volleyball team went to the national championships in 1973, 1974, and 1975, well-to-do parents of players bore the expenses. The first women's scholarship was awarded to volleyball player Jeanne Signell in

1975; she received one quarter's tuition.

"When I started, I had no idea the challenge it would wind up being," said Barbara Palmer, FSU's first full-time athletic director for women. But the players, the coaches, and the administrators persevered – and look at the FSU women's program now!

Towns, businesses, politicians, even athletic programs – all want to be seen as progressive. It's basically the philosophy of "out with the old; in with the new."

In your personal life, that often translates into looking for the latest thing. Your car's running fine, but it's time for a trade-in. Your TV's still delivering a sharp picture, but those HDTV's are really something. And somebody's always putting out a computer that's the fastest thing on the market.

Even God has given us the new to enhance the old in the new covenant of hope and salvation through Jesus Christ. God's new covenant is built upon older promises he had made and marks the culmination of his plan for the redemption of us all. That's why you don't need to get caught waiting around for a new, improved version to hit the market. It just doesn't get any better than the promises of the new covenant God made to you through Jesus.

The difference between the old ballplayer and the new ballplayer is the jersey. The old ballplayer cared about the name on the front. The new ballplayer cares about the name on the back.
-- Former major leaguer Steve Garvey

No matter how old it is,
it just doesn't get any better than
God's new covenant through Jesus Christ.

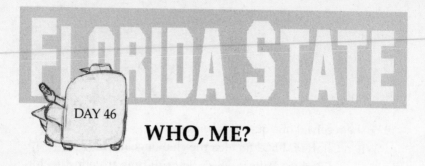

WHO, ME?

Read Judges 6:11-23.

"'But Lord,' Gideon asked, 'how can I save Israel? My clan is the weakest in Manasseh, and I am the least in my family'" (v. 15).

Who, me? That pretty much was senior quarterback Steve Tensi's reaction to a call coach Bill Peterson made in the 1964 game against Georgia.

Tensi led the Seminoles to their greatest season ever to that point in 1964, a 9-1-1 record that included victories over Miami, TCU, Kentucky, Georgia, N.C. State, Florida (for the first time ever), and Oklahoma in the Gator Bowl. That season Tensi threw for 1,683 yards and fourteen touchdowns.

Against Georgia, the Seminoles trailed 14-10 with only eight minutes left to play and faced a fourth and one. Peterson sent a player into the huddle with a play, and he said to Tensi, "Coach wants you to run a quarterback sneak."

Tensi didn't hide his surprise. He recalled that he "looked at [the teammate who brought in the play] and said 'What?'" The player replied, "Quarterback sneak." "Yeah, right," Tensi said. The Seminole quarterback was shocked for a simple reason: He never ran the ball. "I probably ran the ball three times during my entire career. I was stunned he called a quarterback sneak at such a critical time in the game."

When he recovered from his shock, Tensi decided there was

no way he was going to run a sneak. So he called a play he was sure would work much better than the strange one his coach had called: a pass to All-American receiver Fred Biletnikoff. The two connected for the first down, and the Noles moved down the field until Biletnikoff caught a 20-yard touchdown pass to win the game 17-14.

"Peterson didn't say anything to me when I got to the sideline," Tensi said. "If the play hadn't worked, I'm sure he would have said something. But it worked."

Who, me? You probably know exactly how Steve Tensi felt.

How about that time the teacher called on you when you hadn't done a lick of homework? Or the night the hypnotist pulled you out of a room full of folks to be his guinea pig? You know the look on your face and the sinking feeling in your stomach. You've had it when you were suddenly singled out and found yourself in a situation you neither sought nor were prepared for.

You may feel the same way Gideon did about being called to serve God in some way, quailing at the notion of being audacious enough to teach Sunday school, coordinate a high school prayer club, or lead a small group study. After all, who's worthy enough to do anything like that?

The truth is that nobody is – but that doesn't seem to matter to God. And it's his opinion, not yours, that counts.

God doesn't want your ability; instead, He wants your availability.
-- Bobby Bowden

You're right in that no one is worthy to serve God,
but the problem is that doesn't matter to God.

DAY 47

THE BODY BEAUTIFUL

Read 1 Corinthians 6:12-20.

"Do you not know that your body is a temple of the Holy Spirit, who is in you, whom you have received from God? . . . Honor God with your body" (vv. 19, 20b).

Eight years old and LeRoy Butler was restricted to a wheelchair and leg braces.

This was the same LeRoy Butler who was a three-year starter as a defensive back from 1987-89 and was an All-American safety in 1989 for the Seminoles. The same LeRoy Butler who played twelve years with the Green Bay Packers and was All-Pro five times.

Butler was born so pigeon-toed that when he was eight months old, doctors broke bones in both feet so he might stand a chance of walking. It didn't work. When he was six, Butler was fitted with leg braces and confined to a wheelchair.

He spent most of his time at a window of his family's Jacksonville apartment watching other kids play ball. "There'd be 500 or 600 kids playing, and all he could do was watch," his uncle, Charles Durham, said. "He'd go out there once in a while and try to run and would trip all over himself." Durham knew the importance of instilling positive thoughts in a child's head but confessed "deep inside most of us never believed his legs would heal."

What eventually happened was something right out of *Forrest Gump*, who wore the same kind of braces that Butler did. When

SEMINOLES

LeRoy was eight, his older sister, Vicki, accidentally knocked him out of his wheelchair. Butler's leg braces flew off, and he got up and walked without struggling. "All of a sudden, he could run like the wind," said his mother. Butler went right outside and joined his first kickball game.

Your body may never have given you the problems LeRoy Butler's did, but most of us still don't see a body beautiful when we look into a mirror. Too heavy, too short, too pale, too gray — there's always something wrong. In part, though, that's because we compare ourselves to an impossible, illusory standard that Hollywood and fashion magazines have created, and we are inevitably disappointed.

Despite your displeasure, God himself must have been quite partial to your body, because he personally fashioned it and gave it to you free of charge. Your body, like everything else in your life, is thus a gift from God.

But God didn't stop there. He quite voluntarily chose to inhabit your body, sharing it with you in the person of the Holy Spirit. What an act of consummate ungratefulness it is then to abuse your God-given body by violating God's standards for living. To do so is in fact to dishonor God.

If you don't do what's best for your body, you're the one who comes up on the short end

-- Julius Erving

You may not have a fine opinion of your body, but God thought enough of it to personally create it for you.

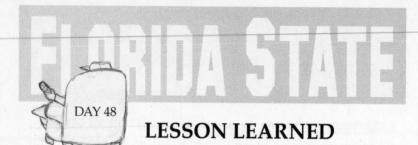

DAY 48

LESSON LEARNED

Read Matthew 11:20-30.

"Take my yoke upon you and learn from me" (v. 29).

Bobby Bowden learned a quite valuable lesson from legendary Georgia Tech coach Bobby Dodd, one that he put into play under trying circumstances in November 1976.

Bowden once said that a game against North Texas State his first year at FSU was "probably my all-time favorite game in 28 years." The Noles were only 3-6 when they headed into Denton and were underdogs.

That was bad enough, but the situation got worse when the boys from the Sunshine State awoke the Saturday morning of game day to discover that five inches of snow had fallen during the night. Bowden polled his players and learned that about 80 percent of them were seeing snow for the first time in their lives. So the coach put the lesson he learned from Dodd into action. In his pregame speech, he said, "There's nothing we can do about this but have fun."

The highlight of the game came when Kurt Unglaub, who, Bowden said, "goes down in history as one of the slowest receivers we ever had," caught a pass and "went slip-slidin' away" for a 91-yard touchdown run. Unglaub kept running all the way out of the end zone because he couldn't see the lines and he wanted to be sure he had the touchdown.

FSU trailed 20-13 with just over two minutes left when Jeff

SEMINOLES

Leggett scored on a seven-yard run and running back Larry Key hit Unglaub with a pass for the two-point conversion. FSU won 21-20.

Bowden reinforced the lesson he had learned from Dodd – always to encourage his players to have fun – by leading his players and his coaches on a postgame roll down a snow bank.

Learning about anything in life requires a combination of education and experience. Education is the accumulation of facts that we call knowledge; experience is the acquisition of wisdom and discernment, which add purpose and understanding to our knowledge.

The most difficult way to learn is trial and error: dive in blindly and mess up. The best way to learn is through example coupled with a set of instructions: Someone has gone ahead to show you the way and then written down all the information you need to follow.

In teaching us the way to live godly lives, God chose the latter method. He set down in his book the habits, actions, and attitudes that make for a way of life in accordance with his wishes. He also sent us Jesus to explain and to illustrate.

God teaches us not just how to exist but how to live. We just need to be attentive students.

It's what you learn after you know it all that counts.

— John Wooden

God has provided the instruction for us to live the godly life he desires for us; we just have to be good students.

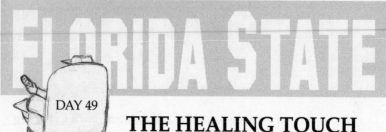

DAY 49

THE HEALING TOUCH

Read Matthew 17:14-20.

"'If you have faith as small as a mustard seed, you can say to this mountain, 'Move from here to there' and it will move. Nothing will be impossible for you'" (v. 20).

Nothing medical technology could do could ease the pain that kept Adrian Crawford from playing basketball for FSU. But God could – and did.

Chronic pain from tendonitis in his left knee shortened Crawford's junior season of 1999-2000. The pain got so intense he couldn't even drive a car, so he called it quits midway through the season, expecting never to play again. After all, he had tried everything medical science had to offer.

But FSU football players Corey Simon and Peter Boulware had another option for him. They urged him to attend a conference in Nashville in July 2000; a faith-healing session was to be part of the event. "I was a skeptic at first," Crawford admitted. He was desperate, though, and so he went up on a stage and let four strangers lay their hands on his left knee and pray for delivery from pain.

"I didn't feel like there was this great sensation in my body," Crawford said. "But maybe 20 minutes later, there was something in my head that told me, 'You're fine.'"

He returned to Tallahassee the next night, went straight to the gym, and played an hour of pain-free basketball. He then played in all 30 games of the 2000-01 season, averaging 26 minutes and 10.4 points per game.

Crawford knows some scoff at the notion of faith healing. "People can reason with me, or argue with me," he said, "but I know what happened. I believe."

What happened is that God healed him.

If we believe in miraculous healing at all, we have pretty much come to consider it to be a relatively rare occurrence. All too often, our initial reaction when we are ill or hurting is to call a doctor rather than to pray. Adrian Crawford's skepticism is our own. If we really want to move a mountain, we'll round up some heavy-duty earthmoving equipment rather than heed the words of Jesus about the power of prayer.

The truth is, though, that divine healing occurs with astonishing regularity; the problem is our perspective. We are usually quite effusive in our thanks to and praise for a doctor or a drug without pausing to consider that God is the one responsible for all healing.

We should also remember that "natural" healing occurs because our bodies react as God created them to. Those healings, too, are divine; they, too, are miraculous. Faith healing is really nothing more – or less – than giving credit where credit is due.

If faith healing is what it took (to heal Adrian Crawford), it's cool.
-- FSU basketball trainer Sam Lunt

**God does in fact heal continuously everywhere;
all too often we just don't notice.**

DAY 50

UNDERDOG

Read 1 Samuel 17:17-50.

"David said to the Philistine, . . . 'This day the Lord will hand you over to me, and I'll strike you down'" (vv. 45-46).

You guys line up alphabetically by height." This is one of the more famous malaprops attributed to FSU's legendary football coach Bill Peterson, who once used the biblical tale of David and Goliath to motivate his team, telling it as only Peterson could.

Hubert Mizell once wrote, "Bill Peterson achieved his purpose in life, to be a stand-up football coach. He also was, unintentionally, a stand-up comedian."

It is unfortunate that history perhaps remembers Peterson for his mangled syntax instead of for his coaching genius. He coached the Seminoles from 1960-70 to a record of 62-41-11, making him the second winningest coach in FSU history. He led the Noles to four bowl games and their first win over Florida during the superb 9-1-1 season of 1964.

Peterson earned the reputation that got him a job in the pros by developing game plans that showcased the passing and catching abilities of the likes of Steve Tensi, Fred Biletnikoff, Kim Hammond, and Ron Sellers.

To inspire his team, Peterson told the David and Goliath story his way: "David needed some help, and he went out and got this sling and some rocks, and he practiced. Just like you guys, he

SEMINOLES

didn't like to practice, but he kept at it. David just went out there and practiced and practiced and practiced, slinging those rocks at tin cans and old beer bottles for days and days and days."

He also once told his team, "I'm the coach around here, and don't you remember it."

Yes, he was.

You probably don't gird your loins, pick up a slingshot and some smooth, round river rocks, and go out to battle ill-tempered giants. You do, however, fight each day to make some economic and social progress and to keep the ones you love safe, sheltered, and protected.

Armed only with your pluck, your knowledge, your wits, and your hustle, in many ways you are an underdog; the best you can hope for is that the world is indifferent. You need all the weapons you can get.

How about using the ultimate weapon David had: the absolute, unshakable conviction that when he tackled opposition of any size, he would prevail. He knew this because he did everything for God's glory and therefore God was in his corner. If you imitate David's lifestyle by glorifying God in everything you do, then God is there for you when you need him. Who's the underdog then?

Always remember that Goliath was a 40-point favorite over Little David.

-- Shug Jordan

**Living to glorify God is the lifestyle
of a champion.**

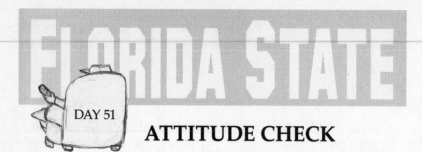

DAY 51

ATTITUDE CHECK

Read 1 Thessalonians 5.

"Give thanks in all circumstances, for this is God's will for you in Christ Jesus" (v. 18).

Jon Nance could have been one of the greatest noseguards in the history of FSU football. His coach, Chuck Amato, said so. He "could have been." If the measure of a player were his attitude, though, Nance would have been.

Nance played only one full season. He lost the 1989 season to academics and then played in key situations in 1990. A hamstring injury cost him the 1991 season. Healthy in 1992, he flashed the greatness Amato and others predicted for him. He finished sixth on the team in tackles and was so good that he was counted on to be the backbone of the line in 1993.

Then, in the spring, a benign tumor the size of a tennis ball was removed from his shoulder. The effects of radiation treatments kept him off the practice field. When the season began, he was healthy and playing the way the coaches expected. So he tore up a knee and had surgery, missing much of his senior season.

After all that, what was Nance's attitude as he prepared for the national championship game against Nebraska, the last time he would wear the garnet and gold? "I feel like I'm blessed," he said. "I've been through so much and I'm still playing. I'd say that's a blessing, a pretty big blessing."

"It's just amazing what he's been through," Amato said. "And he still had that positive attitude."

The players appreciated Nance's attitude, awarding him the 1993 Bob Crenshaw Award, given to the player "with the biggest heart."

How's your attitude? You can fuss because your house is not as big as some, because a coworker talks too much, or because you have to take pills every day. Or you can appreciate your home for providing warmth and shelter, the co-worker for the lively conversation, and the medicine for keeping you reasonably healthy.

Whether life is endured or enjoyed depends largely on your attitude. An attitude of thankfulness to God offers you the best chance to get the most out of your life because living in gratitude means you choose joy in your life no matter what your circumstances.

This world does not exist to satisfy you, so chances are it will not. To trust that the world will provide what you need for a blessed and satisfied life is to choose a path that leads inevitably to frustration and disappointment. True contentment and joy are found in a deep, abiding relationship with God, and the proper attitude with which to approach God is not with haughtiness or anger but with gratitude for all he has given you.

I became an optimist when I discovered that I wasn't going to win any more games by being anything else.
-- Former major league manager Earl Weaver

**Your attitude goes a long way toward
determining the quality of your life
and your relationship with God.**

DAY 52

TOWEL THROWING

Read Numbers 13:25-14:4.

"The men who had gone up with him said, 'We can't attack those people; they are stronger than we are'"
(v. 13:31).

Latavia Coleman was through with FSU basketball; she had quit. But something happened.

In the summer of 1997 before her sophomore season, Coleman, the first freshman to lead the Seminoles in both scoring and rebounding since Sue Galkantas back in 1980-81, had had enough. To her dismay and disappointment, FSU changed coaches for the second time in two years. Coleman told her friends, her teammates, and even her family that she wasn't going to play basketball for FSU anymore.

History shows that Coleman was honored in 2007 as an ACC Legend. A four-year starter for the Noles, she twice made the All-ACC second team. She finished her FSU career as the school's fifth-leading scorer despite missing most of her junior year with a torn ACL, fifth all-time in scoring average at 15.7 points per game, and tenth all-time in rebounds.

So obviously, Coleman didn't follow through on her plans to quit. What happened? Several things did – including God.

Slowly, Coleman changed her mind after she listened to her teammates and she met the new coach, Sue Semrau. But then God stepped in to give her total peace about her change of heart.

SEMINOLES

As the fall semester of 1997 began, Coleman was saved, and God removed everything negative in her life, including her dissatisfaction with basketball. "You feel different as a person," she said. Playing basketball had "seemed like a job. I had to do it. Now it's fun. I'm just enjoying it now, having a ball."

And thanking God every day that she did not quit.

Remember that time you quit a high-school sports team? Bailed out of a relationship? Walked away from that job with the goals unachieved? Sometimes quitting is the most sensible way to minimize your losses, so you may well at times in your life give up on something or someone.

In your relationship with God, however, you should remember the people of Israel, who quit when the Promised Land was theirs for the taking. They forgot one fact of life you never should: God never gives up on you.

That means you should never, ever give up on God. No matter how tired or discouraged you get, no matter that it seems your prayers aren't getting through to God, no matter what – quitting on God is not an option. He is preparing a blessing for you, and in his time and not yours, he will bring it to fruition -- if you don't quit on him.

The first time you quit, it's hard. The second time, it gets easier. The third time, you don't even have to think about it.

-- Bear Bryant

Whatever else you give up on in your life, don't give up on God; he will never, ever give up on you.

DAY 53

A GENTLEMAN PLAYER

Read John 2:13-22.

"He made a whip out of cords, and drove all from the temple area . . .; he scattered the coins of the money changers and overturned their tables" (v. 15).

Charlie Ward is deservedly recognized as one of the greatest athletes in Florida State history, but those who knew him when he was at FSU valued him for something even more important than his athletic skills: Charlie Ward was a gentleman.

Ward, of course, is a Seminole legend, the only Heisman-Trophy winner in collegiate history to play in the NBA, an All-American quarterback who set nineteen school and seven ACC records and led the Noles to their first football national title.

But he was also a consummately nice guy who cared about others. When he was a senior, the mother of a freshman recruit, a police officer, was killed in the line of duty. Ward went to Coach Bobby Bowden and asked that the recruit, Warrick Dunn, be made his roommate so he could look after him.

As Rick Reilly wrote in *Sports Illustrated*, Charlie Ward "doesn't smoke, drink, swear, pierce, cheat, [or] chew." "Every reporter, ankle-taper and drive-thru box gets a 'Sir' or a 'Ma'am'" from him. Reilly said that with Ward, "hopelessly outdated concepts like respect and decency" are cool again.

Even though he quietly slipped in and out of class, one professor said Ward was clearly a role model for other students:

"Nobody leaves the classroom until Charlie does."

Ward was aware that being a gentleman marked him as somewhat different. "Being a real straight arrow is something that a lot of people are offended by, I guess," he said. "But that's the way I've been all my life."

A calm, caring manner and a soft voice are often mistaken for weakness, and gentle men are frequently misunderstood by those who fail to appreciate their inner strength and character. But Charlie Ward's athletic career and Jesus' rampage through the Jerusalem temple illustrate the very real perils of underestimating a determined gentleman.

A gentleman treats other people kindly, respectfully, and justly, and conducts himself ethically in all situations. A gentleman doesn't lack resolve or backbone. Instead, he determines to live in a way that is exceedingly difficult in our selfish, me-first society; he lives the lifestyle God desires for us all.

Included in that mode of living is the understanding that the best way to have a request honored is to make it civilly, with a smile. God works that way, too. He could bully you and boss you around; you couldn't stop him. But instead, he gently requests your attention, waiting for the courtesy of a reply.

Play to win, observe the rules, and act like a gentleman.
-- Legendary basketball coach and author Claire Bee

God is a gentleman, soliciting your attention
politely and then patiently waiting for you
to give him the courtesy of a reply.

DAY 54

PIONEER SPIRIT

Read Luke 5:1-11.

So they pulled their boats up on shore, left everything and followed him (v. 11).

Remember Bob Harbison? Or Jamie Kaplan? How about Ken Misner? They were among the pioneers who blazed a trail at FSU for others to follow.

Harbison was FSU's first-ever Seminole golf coach (1948-52). Kaplan was the first Seminole women's tennis player to earn an NCAA postseason bid (1983), and Misner was FSU's first cross-country All-America (1969-70).

In 1981, Darien Andreau became FSU's first women's cross-country All-America. Among the greatest of the early Seminole women's athletes was Marita Payne, who twenty-one times was named All-America during her track and field career at FSU from 1981 to '84. The first Seminole women's basketball star was Sue Galkantas. From 1981 to '84, she led the team in field goals, free throws, and scoring all four years. She set the school record for career points – 2,323 – and career scoring average – 19.4 ppg.

Roger Slater was another pioneer for the Noles, the first swimming- and-diving All-America in Seminole history (1950 and '51). A whole team of trailblazers began play in 1995 when FSU fielded its first soccer team, led by freshman Melissa Juhl.

And FSU fans should never forget these guys: ends Jim Costello and Chris Banakas, tackles D.L. Middlebrooks and Leonard

Gilberg, guards Jack Tully and Bill Quigley, center Buddy Bryant, quarterback Don Grant, halfbacks Ralph Chaudron and Red Parrish, and fullback Jack Watson. They were the starters in FSU's first-ever football game in 1947.

FSU's sports history is full of pioneers who stepped out to meet new challenges and set standards at which others could aim.

Going to a place in your life you've never been before requires a willingness to take risks and face uncertainty head-on. You may have never helped start a new sports program at a major college, but you've had your moments when your latent pioneer spirit manifested itself. That time you changed careers, ran a marathon, volunteered at a homeless shelter, or went back to school.

While attempting new things invariably begets apprehension, the truth is that when life becomes too familiar and too comfortable, it gets boring. The same is true of God, who is downright dangerous because he calls us to be anything but comfortable as we serve him. He summons us to continuously blaze new trails in our faith life, to follow him no matter what.

Stepping out on faith is risky all right, but the reward is a life of accomplishment, adventure, and joy that cannot be equaled anywhere else.

Life is an adventure. I wouldn't want to know what's going to happen next.

-- Bobby Bowden

Unsafe and downright dangerous, God calls us out of the place where we are comfortable to a life of adventure and trailblazing in his name.

DAY 55

PRESSURE COOKER

Read 1 Kings 18:16-40.

"Answer me, O Lord, answer me, so these people will know that you, O Lord, are God" (v. 37).

You would think Myssi Calkins would have felt the pressure of replacing one of the Seminoles' greatest softball players ever as she headed into her senior season. But once you've been thrown through a car window and survived as Calkins had, then softball offered no pressure at all.

On May 25, 1995, Calkins was asleep in the passenger seat of a vehicle cruising down I-10 in Okaloosa County. She thus didn't see it coming, but the car flipped three times, and Calkins was thrown through a window onto the interstate where she lost consciousness. She survived, not even breaking any bones, but her brush with death changed her life.

For one thing, she drew closer to God, eventually marrying a church pastor. For another thing, softball became fun. The crash "made me enjoy softball more because it's not the most important thing in my life," Calkins said. "I know now how precious life is and softball is one of those things I've been blessed with a chance to play. It's a game."

Still, she faced the challenge of replacing Shama Wilson in the leadoff spot. Wilson was a first-team All-America in 1996 and was described as "FSU's most complete player ever."

So how did Calkins do? Quite nicely, thank you. She led the

1997 ACC champions in batting average (.374), hits, runs, and stolen bases, the last three in FSU's all-time top-ten records for a season. She finished with the school and ACC record for career stolen bases and was a second-team All-America. Pressure? What pressure?

You live every day with pressure. As Elijah did so long ago, you lay it on the line with everybody watching. Your family, co-workers, or employees – they depend on you. You know the pressure of a deadline, of a job evaluation, of taking the risk of asking someone to go out with you, of facing the day-to-day dangers of deployment in a combat zone, of driving in rush-hour traffic.

Help in dealing with both the ordinary and the not-so-ordinary pressures of daily living is readily available, and the only price you pay for it is your willingness to believe. God will give you the grace to persevere if you ask prayerfully.

And while you may need some convincing of this, the pressures you inevitably face each day are in actuality small potatoes because they all will pass. The real pressure comes in deciding where you will spend eternity because that decision is forever. You can handle that pressure easily enough by deciding for Jesus. Eternity is then taken care of; the pressure's off – forever.

Pressure is for tires.

-- Charles Barkley

**The greatest pressure you face in life
concerns where you will spend eternity,
which can be dealt with by deciding for Jesus.**

DAY 56

GOAL ORIENTED

Read 1 Peter 1:3-9.

"For you are receiving the goal of your faith, the salvation of your souls" (v. 9).

The goals of Florida State's football program sure changed over the years of the lengthy Bobby Bowden regime.

When Bowden arrived in Tallahassee in 1976, the initial goal was pretty straightforward: It was to just "beat somebody," he said. It took four games, but in the first home game of the season, the Seminoles beat Kansas State 20-10.

"After we beat somebody and went 5-6 in 1976, we said, 'Gee. If we could just have a winning season,'" Bowden said. So in 1977 the Noles were 8-2 headed into the last game of the season; the goal changed again: Have a winning season *and* beat Florida. The 1977 team closed out the season by blasting Florida 37-9 at Florida Field.

Well, could we just get a bowl bid? After the 1977 season, the 9-2 Noles were invited to the Tangerine Bowl in Orlando and whipped Texas Tech 40-17.

So the goal then became all those other things plus a top-ten ranking and a *major* bowl bid. Those two were achieved in 1979 when the fourth-ranked Noles went to the Orange Bowl and lost to Oklahoma.

Well, then, could we just *win* a major bowl? This one had to wait until 1987 when the third-ranked Noles defeated Nebraska

31-28 in the Fiesta Bowl.

That left only the two biggest goals of all: If we could just have a perfect season and win the national championship! 1993 and 1999 were both championship seasons and 1999 was the perfect season.

The Seminoles have achieved goals only a few other football programs can match.

What are your goals for your life? Have you ever thought them out? Or do you just shuffle along living for your paycheck and whatever fun you can seek out instead of pursuing some greater purpose?

Now try this one: What is the goal of your faith life? You go to church to worship God. You read the Bible and study God's word to learn about God and how God wants you to live. But what is it you hope to achieve? What is all that stuff about? For what purpose do you believe that Jesus Christ is God's son?

The answer is actually quite simple: The goal of your faith life is your salvation, and this is the only goal in life that matters. Nothing you will ever seek is as important or as eternal as getting into Heaven and making sure that everybody you know and love will be there too one day.

I want to win every game and have the best football team in the United States.

-- Bobby Bowden

The most important goal of your life is to get to Heaven and by proclaiming Jesus to help as many people as you can to get there too.

DAY 57

STRANGE BUT TRUE

Read 1 Corinthians 1:18-31.

"The message of the cross is foolishness to those who are perishing, but to us who are being saved it is the power of God" (v. 18).

Dave Cowens is one of the greatest men's basketball players in ACC history, which is strange since Florida State didn't join the ACC until more than twenty years after Cowens graduated.

The FSU men's basketball media guide declares that Cowens is considered to this day to be the greatest player in school history. As a senior center in 1970, he was FSU's first All-America; in 1968, he led the Noles to their first-ever appearance in the NCAA Tournament. That season he set the school record for rebounds: 456. Cowens also holds the school career record for rebounds with 1340 (17.2 per game). In addition, he holds the FSU record for double-doubles in a season (23) and a career (65).

When Cowens played, FSU was an independent, not affiliated with any league. After he graduated, the Noles joined the Metro Conference before changing addresses again, moving over to the Atlantic Coast Conference in 1991. This was, of course, long after Cowens had finished not only his college career at FSU, but also his pro career with the Boston Celtics.

Yet, on ACC Legends Day in March 2005, he was introduced as an Atlantic Coast Conference Legend. "Yeah," Cowens agreed. "It's kind of a misnomer for me. The ACC for me were the guys we wanted to upset because we were independents." Cowens wasn't alone in being strangely claimed as one of its own by the ACC. Rick Barry, who like Cowens was named one of the NBA's all-time top 50 players, represented Miami, which joined the league years after FSU did.

Life is just strange, isn't it? How else to explain the college bowl situation, tattoos, curling, tofu, and teenagers? Isn't it strange that today we have more ways to stay in touch with each other yet are losing the intimacy of personal contact? Who could ever explain Dr. Phil, Christopher Walken, the presidential primaries, and the appeal of Scientology to anyone with even a modicum of what passes for good sense?

And how strange is it that God let himself be killed by being nailed to a couple of pieces of wood? Think about that: the creator and ruler of the entire universe suffering the indignity and the torture of being labeled a common criminal and then executed in the manner reserved for the most ignominious of offenders.

But there's more. The cross, a symbol of disgrace, defeat, and death, ultimately became a worldwide symbol of hope, victory, and life. That's really strange.

So is the fact that love drove God to that cross. It's strange – but it's true.

It may sound strange, but many champions are made champions by setbacks.

-- Olympic champion Bob Richards

It's strange but true: God allowed himself to be killed on a cross because of his great love for you.

ONE TOUGH COOKIE

Read 2 Corinthians 11:21b-29.

"Besides everything else, I face daily the pressure of my concern for all the churches" (v. 28).

He's got a hundred pounds of meanness that don't show."

So said Ted "Satchmo" Martin about teammate Jack Tully, who was listed at 6-feet, 185 pounds when he suited up for the Seminole football team. That would be the first FSU football team in history. Tully was there at the beginning on Oct. 18, 1947, present at midfield as the first elected captain for the first coin toss.

Tully was considered a tough guy by his teammates. "He was a fighter and a leader," teammate Don Grant said of the guard on FSU's groundbreaking football team. "To put it bluntly, nobody was scared of each other," Tully once said. "We played hard. It was who could beat whose backside."

Tully joined the Navy at 17 and served in France in 1944. He then fought in the South Pacific, including Okinawa. When the war ended, his ship docked in Miami where he intended to play football. But then FSU decided to start its own program after its transition from a women's college. A graduate of Leon High, Tully decided to come back home. He went to school on the GI Bill with no football scholarship.

A single incident after Tully graduated propelled his toughness to legendary status. He was a bouncer in Tallahassee when he forcefully escorted a University of Illinois baseball player outside and contributed to the rowdy's education with a few well-placed licks. The man was future Green Bay Packer Ray Nitschke, one of pro football's most feared players during his career.

You don't have to be a legendary FSU offensive lineman to be tough. In today's America, toughness isn't restricted to physical accomplishments and brute strength. Life today demands a different breed of toughness entirely.

Going to work every morning even when you aren't well, sticking by your rules for your children in a society that ridicules parental authority, making hard decisions about the care of your aging parents, often over their objections — you've got to be tough every day just to live honorably, decently, and justly.

Living faithfully requires toughness too, though in America chances are you won't be imprisoned, stoned, or flogged this week for your faith as Paul was. Still, contemporary society exerts subtle, psychological, daily pressures on you to turn your back on your faith and your values. Popular culture promotes atheism, promiscuity, and gutter language; your children's schools have kicked God out; the corporate culture advocates amorality before the shrine of the almighty dollar.

You have to hang tough to keep the faith.

Winning isn't imperative, but getting tougher in the fourth quarter is.
— Bear Bryant

Life demands more than mere physical toughness;
you must be spiritually tough too.

DAY 59

IN THE BAD TIMES

Read Philippians 1:3-14.

"What has happened to me has really served to advance the gospel. . . . Most of the brothers in the Lord have been encouraged to speak the word of God more courageously and fearlessly" (vv. 12, 14).

It was "one of the lowest periods of my life." The life was Bobby Bowden's, and "it" was 1974 when he was the head football coach at West Virginia.

Some anonymous pranksters helped change the history of college football that year when they hanged the football coach in effigy. Bowden's overall record at West Virginia was 42-26, but the 1974 season "became a career pothole that was treated as a sinkhole by critics" when the Mountaineers went 4-7 that year.

Bowden couldn't recall what specifically led critics "to dangle a dummy bearing his name from a tree limb about a block from the stadium" but it wasn't an isolated act. "There were editorials in the student newspaper saying I ought to go," Bowden recalled. "I saw sheets hanging out of dorm windows with 'Bye-bye, Bobby' written on them." Rendering Bowden's situation more precarious than most was a West Virginia state law that limited contracts to one year.

Bowden's Mountaineers rebounded with a nine-win season in 1975, including a win over North Carolina State in the Peach Bowl. He was the toast of Morgantown again, but he hadn't forgotten the awful time his critics had put him through. When Bowden came to Tampa after the season to coach an all-star game, FSU's athletic director contacted him and asked if he'd be interested in coming to Tallahassee.

And so began FSU's good times – in part because of Bobby Bowden's bad times.

Loved ones die. You're downsized. Your biopsy looks cancerous. Your spouse could be having an affair. Maybe incensed critics are hanging you in effigy. Hard, tragic times are as much a part of life as breath.

This applies to Christians too. Faith in Jesus Christ does not exempt anyone from pain. Jesus promises he will be there for us to lead us through the valleys; he never promises that we will not enter them.

The question therefore becomes how you handle the bad times. You can buckle to your knees in despair and cry, "Why me?" Or you can hit your knees in prayer and ask, "What do I do with this?"

Setbacks and tragedies are opportunities to reveal and to develop true character and abiding faith. Your faithfulness -- not your skipping merrily along through life without pain -- is what reveals the depth of your love for God.

If I were to say, "God, why me?" about the bad things, then I should have said, "God, why me?" about the good things that happened in my life.

-- *Arthur Ashe*

**Faithfulness to God requires faith even in --
especially in -- the bad times.**

DAY 60

DECIDE FOR YOURSELF

Read John 6:60-69.

"The words I have spoken to you are spirit and they are life. Yet there are some of you who do not believe" (vv. 63b-64a).

Bobby Bowden hated few thing as badly as he did ties, but one time he decided to go for the tie and said it always felt like a win.

On Nov. 26, 1994, the fourth-ranked Florida Gators were about the business of humiliating the seventh-ranked Seminoles 31-3 in Doak Campbell Stadium. With only thirteen minutes left to play, quarterback Danny Kanell figured it couldn't get any worse so he might as well let it fly.

And he did. Kanell attempted 22 passes in the fourth quarter, completing 18 of them for 232 yards. With the Gators suddenly powerless to stop them, FSU went 84, 60, 73, and 60 yards for touchdowns. With 1:45 left, Rock Preston swept four yards for a touchdown that made it a 31-30 game.

Now came the moment of decision for the head coach: Go for the win and risk the greatest comeback in FSU football history or take the tie? Bowden sent out the kicking team. "I can't afford to blow this," the coach said he thought. "This is too good. Let's ensure a tie."

The players agreed. All-American linebacker Derrick Brooks said, "We did something unprecedented. Coach Bowden felt that we battled back so hard he didn't want us to lose. It was just as sweet as a victory." Linebacker Todd Rebol realized FSU got to 31-30 "by a miracle. If we'd gone for two and missed, it would have been the great comeback that almost happened."

Bowden said, "It's a tie, but really it should be among my favorite wins because it felt like a win."

The moment to which you have arrived in your life – this time, this place, this situation right now – is the result of the decisions you have made. Some you made suddenly and frivolously; some you made carefully and deliberately; some were forced upon you.

Perhaps decisions made for frivolous reasons have determined how your life unfolds. You may have discovered, in fact, that some of those spur-of-the-moment decisions have turned out better than your carefully considered ones.

Of all your life's decisions, however, none is more important than one you cannot ignore: What have you done with Jesus? Even in his time, people chose to follow Jesus or to reject him, and nothing has changed; the decision must still be made and nobody can make it for you.

Carefully considered or spontaneous – how you arrive at a decision for Jesus doesn't matter; all that matters is that you get there.

If you make a decision that you think is the proper one at the time, then that's the correct decision.

-- John Wooden

A decision for Jesus may be spontaneous or considered; what counts is that you make it.

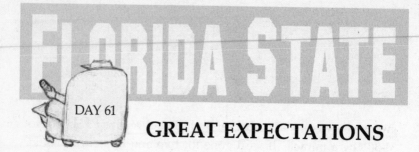

DAY 61

GREAT EXPECTATIONS

Read John 1:43-51.

"'Nazareth! Can anything good come from there?'
Nathanael asked" (v. 46).

One thing Chris Cloer knew he couldn't do when he came to Florida State was fill his brother's tennis shoes.

Chris' older brother was Mat Cloer, who blazed quite a trail on the tennis courts of Tallahassee and throughout the ACC. Mat was FSU's first All-American men's tennis player and was twice the ACC Player of the Year, the first FSU player to win the award.

But Mat was much more for the Seminoles than just a superb player. He was, in fact, a program-changing player. Mat "was kind of the turning-point recruit for us when we got him," said FSU tennis coach Dwayne Hultquist. "He emerged as a top player." As a senior in 2005, Mat led the Noles to the NCAA Elite Eight for the first time in history.

So when Chris started playing for FSU in the spring of 2006, he felt the weight of expectations heaped upon him by his older brother's accomplishments. He heard "oh, that's Mat's brother" quite often. "I've been getting that my whole life," he said. Even Mat was aware of the expectations his accomplishments heaped upon his younger brother. "That bothers me, personally," Mat said. "I'd like to step aside as much as I can and have him take all of the glory. He deserves it."

Chris took it all in stride. "There really wasn't much pressure when I got here," he said. Indeed, he carved out his own niche for the Seminoles rather than attempting to match his brother's legacy. He never challenged for the No. 1 spot, but he won more than 60 singles matches his first three years with the program and was once described as "the heart and soul of this team."

Chris Cloer more than lived up to expectations.

The blind date your friend promised would look like Brad Pitt or Jennifer Aniston but instead resembled a Munster or Cousin Itt. Your vacation that went downhill after the lost luggage. Often your expectations are raised only to be dashed. Sometimes it's best not to get your hopes up; then at least you have the possibility of being surprised.

Worst of all, perhaps, is when you realize that you are the one not meeting others' expectations. The fact is, though, that you aren't here to live up to what others think of you. Jesus didn't; in part, that's why they killed him. But he did meet God's expectations for his life, which was all that really mattered.

Because God's kingdom is so great, God has great expectations for any who would enter, and you should not take them lightly. What the world expects from you is of no importance; what God expects from you is paramount.

Other people may not have had high expectations for me, but I had high expectations for myself.

-- Gymnast Shannon Miller

You have little if anything to gain from meeting the world's expectations of you; you have all of eternity to gain from meeting God's.

DAY 62

A WINNING FORMULA

Read 1 John 1:5-10.

"If we confess our sins, he is faithful and just and will forgive us our sins and purify us from all unrighteousness" (v. 9).

Five straight times FSU had lost to Miami in the Orange Bowl. So as he prepared his team for 1996's game in the graveyard, Coach Bobby Bowden decided on a very particular approach: He kept it simple.

The Noles were 4-0 and ranked no. 3 when they walked onto the turf of the place that had served as the burial ground for their championship hopes in years past. Three times (1988, 1992, 1994) losses in the Orange Bowl had almost certainly cost FSU a chance to play for the national title.

So here they were again, back in that cursed place, playing the sixth-ranked Canes in a game with national title implications. "Everything I heard all week was negative, negative, negative," said junior quarterback Thad Busby, who spent the week of the game receiving reminders of the baleful fate of previous first-time starting Seminole signal callers.

Bowden didn't pretend he wasn't aware of his teams' history in Miami. "I didn't want to let the stadium beat us," he said. So he instructed his team to forget about the ghosts. He told them: "Don't matter if Miami runs out through smoke, don't matter what color uniforms the Hurricanes wear or what happened here in the past. Block and tackle is all. Throw and catch."

So how did that simple formula work? Quite well, thank you. Warrick Dunn ran for 163 yards, Busby passed for 125 yards and didn't make any crucial mistakes, and senior defensive end Reinard Wilson had four sacks. FSU cruised 34-16.

Perhaps the simple life in America was doomed by the arrival of the programmable VCR and the cell phone. Since then, we've been on an inevitably downward spiral into ever more complicated lives.

But we might do well in our own lives to mimic Bobby Bowden's approach to that crucial Miami game. Just remember to block and tackle, throw and catch. In other words, we should approach our life with the keen awareness that success requires simplicity, a sticking to the basics: Revere God, love your family, honor your country, do your best.

Theologians may make what God did in Jesus as complicated as quantum mechanics and the BCS, but God kept it simple for you: believe, trust, and obey. Believe in Jesus as the Son of God, trust that through him God makes possible your deliverance from your sins into Heaven, and obey God in the way he wants you to live.

That's the true winning formula.

I think God made it simple. Just accept Him and believe.
-- Bobby Bowden

Life continues to get ever more complicated,
but God made salvation simple for us
when he showed up as Jesus.

DAY 63

A MOTHER'S LOVE

Read John 19:25-30.

"Near the cross of Jesus stood his mother" (v. 25).

Halina loved her son so much that she sent him away.

Halina Janikowski cried bitterly that day in Poland in 1994 when she put Sebastian, her only child, on a plane for New York City where his father, a former pro soccer player, would meet him. "The farewell at the airport was so difficult," Sebastian's mother recalled later. "Sebastian didn't want to leave me. I told him to go."

In high school in America, Janikowski was a soccer player with such a powerful shot he was offered a $1.8 million contract to turn pro. He declined. He didn't play football until his senior year when word got around high school about the guy with the shaved head and the cannon for a leg. His tryout for football consisted of one kick. He showed up for practice in shorts and sneakers, set a football on a tee at the goal line, took two steps back, and blasted the ball over the head of a coach standing at midfield.

The rule at FSU was that nobody tried to block Janikowski's kicks during practice. That's because in 1998, Seminole defensive back Abdual Howard did block one of Janikowski's rockets in practice. The result left him writhing on the ground in pain with permanent disfigurement of one of his fingers. "Abdual, don't ever do that again," Janikowski said solicitously. "It's going to hurt really bad every time."

Janikowski set FSU and ACC records with 27 field goals in 1998.

SEMINOLES

His 123 points in 1999 were the most scored in a single season in FSU and conference history. He became the first kicker in collegiate history to win back-to-back Lou Groza awards (1998-99), presented to the nation's top collegiate kicker. He was All-ACC and All-America and was drafted in the first round by the Oakland Raiders.

With some of his money, he brought his mother to America.

Mamas often do the sort of thing that Halina Janikowski did for Sebastian: sacrifice personal happiness for the sake of a child. No mother in history, though, has faced a challenge to match that of Mary, chosen by God to be the mother of Jesus, who was God in the flesh. Mary experienced both great joy and unique perplexity in her relationship with her son.

To the end, though, Mary stood by her boy. She followed him all the way to his execution, an act of love and bravery since Jesus was condemned as an enemy of the Roman Empire.

But just as mothers like Mary and Halina – and perhaps yours -- would apparently do anything for their children, so will God do anything out of love for his children. After all, that was God on the cross at the foot of which Mary stood, and he was dying for you, one of his children.

I was a momma's boy.

– Bobby Bowden

Mamas often sacrifice for their children, but God, too, will do anything out of love for his children, including dying on a cross.

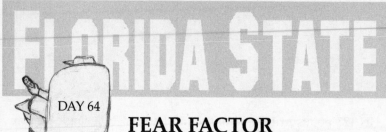

DAY 64

FEAR FACTOR

Read Matthew 14:22-33.

"[The disciples] cried out in fear. But Jesus immediately said to them: 'Take courage! It is I. Don't be afraid'" (vv. 26-27).

As she prepared to run the 60-meter dash in the 2000 NCAA Indoor Championships, Florida State senior Tonya Carter was so afraid that she devised a strategy to conquer her fear. She ran with her eyes closed.

Carter was an All-American sprinter in 1999 and 2000 and the ACC Performer of the Year in 2000. So why was this track and field veteran so afraid at the 2000 Indoors? Because of the expectations that had been placed upon her since she had won the ACC Indoor Championships in February with a run of 7.15 seconds, a school and conference record.

As Carter explained it, "After I ran that 7.15, all eyes were on me. I was really worried about meeting everybody's expectations. It played on my mind a little bit."

So as she lined up in Fayetteville, Ark., on Saturday, March 11, Carter "was extremely scared." She had to do something or her fear would paralyze her. First she prayed. "The last thing that went through my mind was, 'Please, God,'" she said.

Then she did something extremely interesting and rather bizarre. About halfway through the race, she closed her eyes and ran in the dark, never worrying about missing a step. "When you've been sprinting as long as I have," Carter said, "it's kind of mechanical. Just get out and run."

And run she did, even with her eyes closed. God answered her prayer in 7.21 seconds, the time it took Carter to win the race and become the first Lady Seminole since 1985 to win an individual national title.

Some fears are universal; others are particular. Speaking to the Rotary Club may require a heavy dose of antiperspirant. Elevator walls may feel as though they're closing in on you. And don't even get started on being in the dark with spiders and snakes during a thunderstorm.

We all live in fear, and God knows this. Dozens of passages in the Bible urge us not to be afraid. God isn't telling us to lose our wariness of oncoming cars or big dogs with nasty dispositions; these are helpful fears God instilled in us for protection. What God does wish driven from our lives is a spirit of fear that dominates us, that makes our lives miserable and keeps us from doing what we should, such as sharing our faith with others. In commanding that we not be afraid, God reminds us that when we trust completely in him, we find peace that calms our fears.

The Good Lord might not want to take me, but He might be after the pilot.

— *Bobby Bowden on his fear of small planes*

**You have your own peculiar set of fears,
but they should never paralyze you
because God is greater than anything you fear.**

DAY 65

THE SCARS

Read John 20:19-31.

'"Put your finger here; see my hands. Reach out your hand and put it into my side. Stop doubting and believe'" (v. 27).

Chris Weinke bears the scars of his time as a Seminole.

As what was to be the unforgettable 1999 season approached, real doubts swirled as to whether Weinke would be able to play. In 1998, Weinke led the Noles to an 8-1 record and set a school record with 218 passes without an interception before an injury "sabotaged his season and threatened his career."

Against Virginia, Weinke was sacked and his neck was jammed. "I knew I was hurt pretty bad," he said. The next morning X-rays revealed a herniated disk and a bone chip. "The more I heard (from doctors), the more scary it got," head coach Bobby Bowden said. Weinke underwent surgery to fuse two vertebrae and to remove the herniated disk. When he was released from the hospital, everyone breathed sighs of relief.

Within days, though, he was back in the hospital with nausea, dehydration, and debilitating headaches. A spinal fluid leak was discovered, and a second surgery was necessary. He was left with a scar three to four inches long in the front of his neck and another scar eight to ten inches long that reached from the back of his neck to between his shoulder blades.

That surgery freed Weinke from the pain, but left him with

other problems. Seven weeks later, he still had lost more than twenty pounds and "looked wan, even ghostly." As late as the Fiesta Bowl, which he missed, he became dizzy if he moved quickly.

Thus, as the 1999 season neared, doubts surrounded FSU's now-scarred quarterback though doctors had cleared him to play and Weinke had regained his lost weight. The rest, of course, is glorious Seminole history that includes the 1999 national championship and the 2000 Heisman Trophy.

You've got scars too. That car wreck left a good one. So did that bicycle crash. Maybe we better not talk about that time you said, "Hey, watch this!" Your scars are part of your life story, the residue of the pain you've encountered. People's scars are so unique and ubiquitous they're used to identify bodies.

Even the resurrected Jesus proved who he was to a skeptical Thomas by the scars of the nail marks in his hands and his side. How interesting it is that even with his resurrected body, Jesus bore the scars of his torture. Apparently, he bears them still even as he sits upon his throne in Heaven.

Why would he even have them in the first place? Why would he, who had all the power in the universe, submit meekly to being led to slaughter like a lamb?

He did it for you. Jesus' scars tell the story of his love for you.

Pain heals. Chicks dig scars. Glory lasts forever.
-- Keanu Reeves to his teammates in The Replacements

In your scars lie stories; the same is true for Jesus, whose scars tell of his love for you.

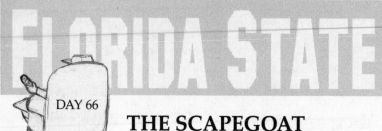

DAY 66

THE SCAPEGOAT

Read Leviticus 16:15-22.

"He is to lay both hands on the head of the live goat and confess over it all the wickedness and rebellion of the Israelites — all their sins — and put them on the goat's head" (v. 21).

Barry Smith admitted he was the goat of a game. But not for long.

Smith was one of FSU's first big-play receivers. From 1970 to 1972, he scored 27 touchdowns and tallied 164 points, both school records at the time. He was first-team All-America in 1972.

Smith was a sophomore in 1970 when the legend of "Huff the Magic Dragon" was born against Florida. Gary Huff made his first collegiate appearance by coming off the bench and throwing three touchdown passes – in the fourth quarter. An inspired alumnus wrote a poem titled "Huff the Magic Dragon." Smith caught a 66-yard touchdown bomb from Huff and thought, "I'm going to like this guy."

He was also present for one of the most famous tackles in FSU history. In the last game of that 1970 season, Houston was waxing the Noles when a Cougar intercepted a pass and took off for yet another touchdown. Coach Bill Parcells started screaming, "Somebody do something!" Linebacker Dan Whitehurst did; he stepped off the sidelines and nailed the Houston player. "The poor guy never knew what hit him," Smith recalled.

The 1971 Kansas game started badly for Smith and FSU. "I probably dropped two or three balls that [Huff] threw to me early in the game," Smith said. "The passes hit me right between the numbers. . . . I was the goat." But he turned it around when he caught an 88-yard touchdown pass, at the time the longest touchdown catch in school history. FSU won 30-7.

A particular type of goat -- a scapegoat – could really be useful. Mess up at work? Bring him in to get chewed out. Make a decision your children don't like? Let him put up with the whining and complaining. Forget your anniversary? Call him in to grovel and explain.

What a set-up! You don't have to pay the price for your mistakes, your shortcomings, and your failures. You get off scot-free. Exactly the way forgiveness works with Jesus.

Our sins separate us from God because we the unholy can't stand in the presence of the holy God. To remove our guilt, God requires a blood sacrifice. Out of his unimaginable love for us, he provided the sacrifice – his own son. Jesus is the sacrifice made for us; through Jesus and Jesus alone, forgiveness and eternity with God are ours.

It's a bumper sticker, but it's true: We aren't perfect; we're just forgiven.

I've been a hero before, and I've been a goat before. I have to admit, I like hero a lot better.

– Bobby Bowden

**For all those times you fail God, you have Jesus
to take the guilt and the blame for you.**

DAY 67

SMALL SEEDS

Read Mark 4:21-32.

"[The Kingdom of God] is like a mustard seed, which is the smallest seed you plant in the ground. Yet when planted, it grows and becomes the largest of all garden plants" (vv. 31-32).

Don Loucks was present at the creation.

In its long and storied history, the Florida State men's basketball program has won more than one thousand games. The Nole men play in the Donald L. Tucker Center, which seats more than 12,000. They play in the Atlantic Coast Conference, the best collegiate basketball conference in the country. The Seminoles are no strangers to winning seasons that earn them invitations to postseason tournaments. At the collegiate level, it just doesn't get any bigger than this.

And "this" is a long way from Dec. 10, 1947, when FSU defeated Spring Hill College 39-36. That was FSU's first-ever basketball win in its first-ever game. It was, in fact, the Seminoles' first-ever win in any intercollegiate sport as the inaugural football team had gone winless. The coach that night was Don Loucks.

To appreciate how the FSU basketball program has grown, consider that on the night of that inaugural win over Spring Hill, Loucks had no assistant coaches, no managers, no trainers, not even a scorekeeper. Head football coach Ed Williamson filled that last role, but he never could verify which player scored FSU's first basket. Loucks said, "[Forward and later Tallahassee mayor] Shad Hilaman always said he did, and I never argued with him." Little doubt exists, however, that the star of that first team was Bill Kratzert, who also starred in football and tennis.

Loucks' team also won the second game it played, whipping Troy State 57-37. The seeds were planted for what would grow into the big-time spectacle that is FSU men's basketball today.

Most worthwhile aspects of life take time and tending to grow from small beginnings into something magnificent. A good marriage is that way. Your beautiful lawn just didn't appear. Old friends get that way after years of cultivation. And children don't get to be responsible and caring adults overnight.

Your faith, too, must be nurtured over time. Remember those older folks you revered as saints when you were growing up? Such distinction is achieved, not awarded. That is, they didn't start out that way. They were mature Christians because they walked and talked with Jesus; they prayed; they studied God's word; they helped others. They nourished and tended their faith with constant, loving care and attention.

In your faith as in other areas of your life, it's OK to start small. Faith is a journey, not a destination. You keep growing as those saints did, always and ceaselessly moving on to bigger and better things in and for God.

Everybody is looking for instant success, but it doesn't work that way. You build a successful life one day at a time.

-- *Lou Holtz*

Faith is a lifelong journey of growth.

GENIUS AT WORK

Read 1 Kings 4:29-34; 11:1-10.

*"Although [God] had forbidden Solomon to follow
other gods, Solomon did not keep the Lord's command"
(v. 11:10).*

60 Divide." It wasn't a compliment.

T.K. Wetherell's first boss at Florida State was his receivers coach, Bobby Bowden. The two reversed roles in 2003 when Wetherell was named FSU's president. For the longtime acquaintances and friends, "60 Divide" was code that went back to 1965 and Wetherell's first varsity game.

60 Divide was a play in which Wetherell lined up as a flanker and ran an out toward the sideline. Wetherell said he practiced that play "all summer long. We must have run it a million times." The play was a guaranteed touchdown. Running back Larry Green would sprint down the middle of the field, and quarterback Kim Hammond would hit him wide open every time.

FSU trailed 7-3 in the fourth quarter in the opener against TCU when the coaching staff called the play. It was a disaster; Wetherell ran into Green, Hammond's pass hit Green in the head, and the TCU cornerback nabbed an interception.

Wetherell recalled, "I come off the field, and I'm thinking, 'That idiot Green ran the wrong route.'" He was about halfway to the sideline when "and I'll never forget this – I look up and Bowden was standing there with his hands on his hips like he does. And he says to me, 'Are you just stupid?'" Then it hit Wetherell. He, not Green, had run the wrong route.

So, Wetherell said, "Every time I do something dumb in this job [as president], I'll get a message. 'Coach Bowden called.' 'What did he say?" '60 Divide.'"

Remember that time you wrecked the car when you dropped hot coffee in your lap? That cold morning you fell out of the boat? The time you gave your honey a tool box for her birthday? Or forgot your anniversary altogether.

Formal education notwithstanding, we all make our share of dumb moves because time spent in a classroom is not an accurate gauge of common sense. Folks impressed with their own smarts often grace us with erudite pronouncements that we intuitively recognize as flawed, unworkable, or simply wrong.

A good example is the observation that great intelligence and scholarship are not compatible with faith in God. That is, the more you know, the less you believe. Any incompatibility occurs, however, only when we begin to trust in our own wisdom rather than the wisdom of God. We forget, as Solomon did, that God is the ultimate source of all our knowledge and wisdom and that even our ability to learn is a gift from God.

Not smart at all.

I don't hire anybody not brighter than I am. If they're not smarter than me, I don't need them.

-- Bear Bryant

Being truly smart means trusting in God's wisdom rather than only in your own knowledge.

THE DANGER ZONE

Read Genesis 3:1-24.

*"So the Lord God banished him from the Garden of Eden
to work the ground from which he had been taken" (v. 23).*

From death threats to players' deaths, in his long career Bobby Bowden knew the dangers of college football and fame.

Pablo Lopez, Michael Hendricks, and Devaughn Darling were all active FSU football players when they died. In 1986, Lopez was shot and killed outside Montgomery Gym; Hendricks died in 1992 from an electrical accident near his home. Darling collapsed and died in February 2001 after an offseason conditioning drill.

Bowden had to break the news of Lopez' death to the players who had rushed to the hospital emergency room when they heard about the shooting. That was tragic enough, but Bowden called Darling's death "the worst thing to happen. . . . We'd never had anything like that." The coroner never determined a conclusive cause of death.

In 1990 shortly before the South Carolina game in Columbia (which FSU won 41-10), a letter arrived in the athletic offices threatening Bowden's life at the next out-of-town game. The letter was passed on to Florida highway patrolman Billy Smith, who oversaw Bowden's security. Smith told Bowden about the threat and vowed to do everything he could to protect the coach.

The veteran patrolman felt that the seriousness of the threat didn't really sink in with Bowden until the game was over and the

SEMINOLES

coach walked out of the dressing room and saw 132 uniformed officers there to escort him to his car. "When I walked out that door and saw all those law enforcement guys, my heart sunk," Bowden said.

Life is inherently dangerous; after all, it always winds up with a death.

The most dangerous thing you can do in life, however, is to rebel against God by not living the way he has told you to. You may well be what the world considers a "good" person. You're not an adulterer, a thief, or a liar; you don't drink excessively, curse (except perhaps when FSU fumbles), gamble, litter, or do drugs. You work hard, care for your family, and are kind to all dogs and most cats.

But it's not the world's opinion that counts. Despite a sober and responsible lifestyle, you may well be rebelling against God even though you never consciously and intentionally decided to do so. Have you accepted Jesus as your savior? As a result, do you pray, read the Bible, speak Jesus' name to others, attend church faithfully, serve God by serving others, and tithe? In other words, are you living a godly life or a worldly one?

God knows which it is, and if it's the latter, you're sitting right square in God's danger zone.

It is very dangerous to have your self-worth riding on your results as an athlete.

-- Tennis pro Jim Courier

Life's greatest danger lies in rebelling against God by not living the way he has told you to.

DAY 70

AS YOU SEE IT

Read John 20:11-18.

"Mary stood outside the tomb crying" (v. 11).

Because FSU's legendary baseball coach Mike Martin had a change in perspective, he once thanked God that the opposing team beat his Seminoles in the national championship game.

Martin is one of the greatest coaches in college baseball history, a member of the coaches hall of fame. Under Martin's guidance, FSU became one of the most prestigious college baseball programs in the country.

Since Martin has won more than 1,500 games, a quite natural assumption may be that winning is his top priority. At one time in his life, it was. Martin's wife, Carol, said, "People used to laugh and call him 'wild man.' He wanted to win so badly."

Martin's life changed in 1986 when the Semioles lost in the national championship game to Arizona 10-2. Martin stood at second base congratulating opposing coach Jerry Kendall when he saw a woman struggling to make her way toward the two coaches. The woman was Kendall's wife, who was dying of Lou Gehrig's disease. "I'll never forget it," Martin said. "She got all the way to second base and hugged Jerry. I was walking off the field, and I just looked up and thanked God" that Kendall, a Christian man, had won.

Kendall's wife died a month later.

"That is when the real turnaround came in my life," Martin

said. "It just put so much in perspective." Pitching coach Jeremy Shouppe said Martin realized there was so much more to life than baseball. "Now his first priority is God and Christ. He lives that every day."

The perspective from which you view life goes a long way toward determining whether you slink through your time on this Earth bowed down by despair, anger, and hopelessness, or you stride boldly through life buoyed by joy and hope.

Mary is a good example of the contrast that perspective offers. On that first Easter morning, she stood by Jesus' tomb crying, her heart broken, because she still viewed life through the perspective of Jesus' death. But how her attitude, her heart, and her life all changed when she saw the morning through the perspective of Jesus' resurrection!

As it is with life, so it is with death. While you can delay it, you can't avoid that inevitable appointment with death. What you can determine is how you perceive it. Is death fearful, dark, fraught with peril and uncertainty, at best an eternal, disquieting lapse into nothingness? Or is it a simple passageway to glory, the light, and loved ones, an elevator ride to paradise?

It's a matter of perspective that depends totally on whether or not you're standing by Jesus' side when death arrives.

I used to say you couldn't take Jesus in the dugout. Nothing could be further from the truth.
— Mike Martin

Whether death is a fearsome enemy or a solicitous chauffeur is a matter of perspective.

HOMEBODIES

Read 2 Corinthians 5:1-10.

"We . . . would prefer to be away from the body and at home with the Lord" (v. 8).

For one incredible stretch, the FSU football team proved to be the ultimate homebodies.

On Sept. 5, 1992, the Seminoles whipped Duke 48-21. That game began a remarkable streak; more than ten years passed before the Noles lost another home game. They went 54 straight games at Doak Campbell Stadium without a loss. The only game they didn't win was the 31-31 tie with Florida in 1994 that featured the Seminoles' most incredible comeback ever. The streak ended on Oct. 13, 2001, with a loss to second-ranked Miami.

Steve Ellis of the *Tallahassee Democrat* described some of the things that happened during the streak.

The Noles rolled up more than 15 miles of total offense and outscored their opponents by 30.7 points per game. Only twice during the streak were they held under 20 points: 17 against Clemson in 1994 (17-0) and 13 against North Carolina in 1996 (13-0).

Only once – against top-ranked Florida in 1996 (24-21) – were the Seminoles the underdog. That was the only time during the streak the goal posts were torn down and was one of twenty victories over top 20 teams and seven wins over top 10 opponents.

During the streak, Seminole fans consumed more than 1,200

SEMINOLES

tons of ice in their soft drinks and more than 1.2 million hot dogs. One person died; a woman suffered a fatal heart attack in 1997. More than 20,000 hours were spent cleaning up Doak Campbell Stadium after games.

For the FSU football team and its fans, there was truly no place like home.

Home is not necessarily a matter of geography. It may be that place you share with your spouse and your children, whether it's Florida or Alaska. You may feel at home when you return to Tallahassee, wondering why you were so eager to leave in the first place. Maybe the home you grew up in still feels like an old shoe, a little worn but comfortable and inviting.

God planted that sense of home in us because he is a God of place, and our place is with him. Thus, we may live our entire lives a few blocks away from our parents and grandparents or we may move to a new town every few years, but we will still sometimes feel as though we don't really belong no matter where we are.

We don't; our true home is with God in the place Jesus has gone ahead to prepare for us. We are homebodies who are not home yet, and so we are perpetually homesick.

Everybody's better at home.
— *Basketball player Justin Dentmon*

We are continually homesick for our real home, which is with God in Heaven.

DAY 72

SEEING THE VISION

Read Acts 26:1, 9-23.

"So then, . . . I was not disobedient to the vision from heaven" (v. 19).

Assistant coach Wayne McDuffie saw something that no other Florida State coaches at the time did: Charlie Ward as a Seminole quarterback.

Had McDuffie not been a stubborn visionary, FSU's first-ever Heisman-Trophy winner probably would never have played a down for the Noles. As the coaches assembled their recruiting class in early 1988, nobody but McDuffie wanted Ward behind the center. "We knew [Ward] was a player," said Brad Scott, who was the recruiting coordinator then. "But could he play quarterback at FSU?"

Bobby Bowden didn't think so. "What I saw was a great running quarterback," he said. Bowden agreed to take Ward "if he'd consent to play another position." But Ward's parents exacted a promise from recruiters McDuffie and John Eason that if their son committed to FSU, it would be as a quarterback.

Part of the problem was that the Seminoles didn't need another quarterback. They were set with Chip Ferguson and Peter Tom Willis battling for the starting job in the spring. Redshirt freshmen Casey Weldon and Brad Johnson were on hand as the future. The coaches were recruiting only one quarterback, and they all favored a drop-back passer from Tampa.

SEMINOLES

Everyone except McDuffie, that is, who envisioned Charlie Ward as one of FSU's greatest quarterbacks. Finally, at a January coaches' meeting, McDuffie launched an impassioned tirade that included beating his fist on a table and standing on a chair and shouting. When he finished, the other coaches yielded to McDuffie's vision and persistence. Charlie Ward would be a Seminole quarterback.

To speak of visions is often to risk their being lumped with palm readings, Ouija boards, seances, horoscopes, and other such useless mumbo-jumbo. The danger such mild amusements pose, however, is very real in that they indicate a reliance on something other than God. It is God who knows the future; it is God who has a vision and a plan for your life. A medium should be a steak and nothing more.

You probably do have a vision for your life, a plan for how it should unfold. It's the dream you pursue through your family, your job, your hobbies, your interests. But your vision inspires a fruitful life only if it is compatible with God's plan. As the apostle Paul found out, you ignore God's vision at your peril. If you pursue it, however, you'll find an even more glorious life than you could ever have envisioned for yourself.

If I could see into the future, I wouldn't be sitting here talking to you doorknobs. I'd be out investing in the stock market
-- Boston Celtic Kevin McHale to reporters

Your grandest vision for the future pales beside the vision God has of what the two of you can accomplish together.

DAY 73

FOOD FOR THOUGHT

Read Acts 10:9-16.

"Then a voice told him, 'Get up Peter. Kill and eat.'
'Surely not, Lord!' Peter replied. 'I have never eaten
anything impure or unclean.' The voice spoke to him a
second time, 'Do not call anything impure that God has
made clean'" (vv. 13-15).

You would think that receiving a football scholarship would merit some sort of celebration. All it got Andre Wadsworth was having his lunch snatched up and tossed into the trash.

A defensive end, Wadsworth was the ACC Defensive Player of the Year and a consensus All-America in 1997. He was the third player taken in the 1998 NFL draft, the highest an FSU player had ever been drafted.

Coming out of high school, though, he was unrecruited, so he decided to walk on at Florida State. He hung on through the glorious 1993 season in which he was redshirted and didn't get to travel with the team. Then before the 1994 season began, Coach Bobby Bowden awarded him a scholarship. The first thing Wadsworth did was call his momma and tell her the news.

The second thing he did was head down to the cafeteria to eat at the training table. Only scholarshipped players could eat at the training table; everyone else had to pay. Wadsworth "told the people at the cash registers that [he] had just been given a scholarship, so they let [him] go ahead and eat." He didn't get

SEMINOLES

to enjoy his turkey sandwich long, though, because the wrath of the cafeteria's director suddenly descended upon him. She strode right up to Wadsworth, grabbed his sandwich, and sailed it into a trash can. "She thought I'd lied to her workers about being on scholarship," Wadsworth said.

Needless to say, that didn't happen again and Wadsworth had no more problems with his chow.

Belly up to the buffet, boys and girls, for barbecue, sirloin steak, grilled chicken, crab legs, and fried catfish with hush puppies. Rachael Ray's a household name; hamburger joints, pizza parlors, and taco stands lurk on every corner; and we have a TV channel devoted exclusively to food. We love our chow.

Food is one of God's really good ideas, but consider the complex divine plan that gets those French fries to your mouth. The creator of all life devised a system in which living things are sustained and nourished physically through the sacrifice of other living things in a way similar to what Christ underwent to save you spiritually. Whether it's fast food or home-cooked, everything you eat is a gift from God secured through a divine plan in which some plants and animals have given up their lives.

Pausing to give thanks before you dive in seems the least you can do.

I have no prejudices when it comes to food. I will eat anything.

-- *Bobby Bowden*

God created a system that nourishes you through the sacrifice of other living things; that's worth a thank-you.

TEACHER'S PET

Read John 3:1-16.

"[Nicodemus] came to Jesus at night and said, 'Rabbi, we know you are a teacher who has come from God'" (v. 2).

Kimmy Carter knew she wanted to play high-school softball; she just didn't know what position. "Why don't you try catching?" an interested party suggested. Considering the source, it was a pretty good idea.

Carter is the daughter of Gary Carter, who spent 18 years as a major-league catcher and in 2003 was elected into the National Baseball Hall of Fame. It was he who thought his daughter might make a pretty good catcher. So she found some of her dad's old gear and put it on. She knew she had found her position when her dad said, "Kimmy, you look just like me behind the plate."

Well, not quite. The equipment was designed for a man 6-foot-2, and Kimmy was "5-foot nothing." "It was so big on her that the shin guards went up midway to her thighs," Gary said. "Seeing her in all of the gear just looked funny."

But there was nothing funny about the way Kimmy played catcher with her dad acting as her teacher. "Anytime I needed help, all I had to do was ask him," she said.

The kid who looked like her dad behind the plate went on to star at FSU, starting all four years from 1999-2002. Three times she was All-ACC; she was the team captain as a senior, and her name is all over the Seminole record book, including the school record for career RBIs.

Gary Carter was proud of his daughter's softball abilities, but there was one part of her life of which he was even prouder. He once said, "From a father standpoint, this is what you're most proud of: She is on fire for the Lord."

You can read this book, break 90 on the golf course, and be successful at your job because somebody taught you. And as you learn, you become the teacher yourself. You teach your children how to play Monopoly and how to drive a car. You show rookies the ropes at the office and teach baseball's basics to a Little League team.

This pattern of transforming from student to teacher includes your spiritual life also. Somebody taught you about Jesus, and this, too, you must pass on. Jesus taught a truth that the religious teachers and the powerful men of his day did not want to hear. Little has changed in that regard, as the world today often reacts to Jesus' message with scorn and disdain.

Nothing, not even death itself, could stop Jesus from teaching his lesson of life and salvation. So should nothing stop you from teaching life's most important lesson: Jesus saves.

The only reason we make good role models is because you guys look up to athletes. . . . The real role models should be your parents and teachers!

-- *NFL player Dante Hall*

In life, you learn and then you teach,
which includes learning and teaching about Jesus,
the most important lesson of all.

DAY 75

NEVER OVER IT

Read Ephesians 2:1-10.

"For it is by grace you have been saved, through faith—and this not from yourselves, it is the gift of God—not by works, so that no one can boast" (vv. 8-9).

Philip Rountree never got over FSU football. When he was 84 years old, decades after he had played his last down, he declared that the memory of playing for FSU "is something no one will ever be able to take away from you."

Rountree was one of the 45 or so players, all former servicemen, who began football at FSU with the first team in 1947. At 24, Rountree, who played halfback, was the oldest of the bunch.

After the war ended and they were discharged, Harold Conrad, Bill Quigley, and E.J. Quigley landed at Newberry College in South Carolina in search of academics and football. Everything started out well, but "when we started registering for classes we noticed something," Conrad recalled. "Everything we had to take was Bible courses." That's when the trio realized they were at a Bible college. They decided they wanted "more football and less religion." They heard about the changes in Tallahassee and came home to make athletic history.

Rountree and Bill Quigley were among the captains for the first game, played on Centennial Field, which had been constructed in 1924 from some fill dirt. In that first-ever game against Stetson, FSU took a 6-0 lead when Don Grant hit Charles McMillan with a 24-yard touchdown pass, but the closest they came to winning that season was a 6-0 loss to Cumberland. "We really thought we could win that one," Conrad said. "It was misty and rainy and 20 degrees. There were about ten people there."

"Those were the days," Bill Quigley said. And those first FSU players never got over them.

Some things in life have a way of getting under your skin and never letting go. Your passion may have begun the first time you rode in a convertible. When you chowed down on your first slice of New-York style pizza. Or when you first saw the one who would become your spouse and you couldn't locate your breath. For sure, you knew you were hooked the first time you walked into Doak Campbell Stadium on game day.

You can put God's love on that list. Once you encounter it in the person of Jesus Christ, you never get over it. That's because when you really and sincerely give your life to Jesus by acknowledging him as the Lord of your life, God's love – his grace – changes you. It releases you from the fear of death's apparent victory and thus frees you to live in peace and in joy.

When you meet Jesus, you're never the same again. You just never get over the experience.

You spend a good deal of your life gripping a baseball, and it turns out it was the other way around all the time.
-- Former pitcher Jim Bouton

Some things hit you so hard you're never the same again; meeting Jesus is like that.

ANSWERING THE CALL

Read 1 Samuel 3:1-18.

"The Lord came and stood there, calling as at the other times, 'Samuel! Samuel!' Then Samuel said, 'Speak, for your servant is listening'" (v. 10).

Buster Posey answered his coach's call, and the result was collegiate greatness.

Posey came to Tallahassee as a shortstop. Legendary Seminole baseball coach Mike Martin knew immediately Posey would be the cornerstone of his team. "From the third or fourth game he played [at shortstop]," Martin said, Posey "didn't play like a freshman." All Posey did was make All-America in 2006 as a freshman shortstop.

The Noles needed a catcher, though, for 2007, and Martin asked his All-America to change positions. Posey answered the coach's call; he put on the catcher's gear and became the first sophomore in collegiate history to be named a finalist for the Johnny Bench Award, given to the nation's top collegiate catcher.

Then came the 2008 season when Posey won the Bench award, the Golden Spikes Award, and the Dick Howser Trophy as the nation's best player and was named player of the year by Collegiate Baseball and *Baseball America*. He won the ACC triple crown and led the nation in batting average, hits, RBIs, total bases, slugging percentage, and on-base percentage.

During that incredible season, Posey answered his coach's call when the team needed him. He doubled as the team's closer, a situation Martin admitted he had never had before. Posey led the team in saves and did not give up an earned run the whole season. In a 10-0 win over Savannah State, Posey became the fourth player in Seminole history to play all nine positions in a game.

Buster Posey answered the call.

A team player is someone like Buster Posey who does whatever the coach calls upon him to do for the good of the team.

Something quite similar occurs when God places a specific call upon a Christian's life. When that happens, God expects an answer from the one he has called, and God is not particularly inclined to take "no" for a reply.

This is a heap scarier, though, than shifting positions on a baseball or football team. That's because of the way many folks understand what answering God's call involves: Going full-time into the ministry, packing the family up, and moving halfway around the world to some place where folks have never heard of air conditioning, fried chicken, baseball, or the FSU Seminoles. Zambia. The Philippines. Cleveland even.

Not for you, no thank you. And who can blame you?

But God usually calls folks to serve him where they are. In fact, God put you where you are right now. Are you serving him there?

It was like being in a foreign country.
-- Welsh soccer player Ian Rush on playing in Italy

**God calls you to serve him right now,
right where he has put you, wherever that is.**

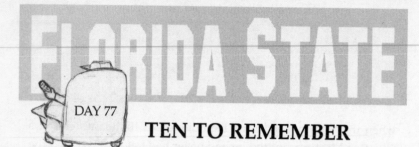

TEN TO REMEMBER

Read Exodus 20:1-17.

"God spoke all these words: 'I am the Lord your God .... You shall have no other gods before me'" (vv. 1, 3).

Not surprisingly, considering their success over the years, the Seminoles have had some real runaways on the football field.

The greatest margin of victory in Florida State football history is 63 points, achieved twice: 66-3 over Louisiana Tech in 1988 and 70-7 over Tulane in 1992. FSU also crunched Tulsa 76-14 in 1985 and N.C. State 77-17 in 1995. The 77 points set a school record as the Seminoles rolled up a downright astounding 745 total yards of offense in the lopsided win. Interestingly, the slaughter came only two weeks after a 70-26 undressing of Duke that prompted Coach Bobby Bowden to write a letter of apology to the Blue Devil head coach for running up the score.

Florida State has won five games by 59 points: 59-0 over Louisville in 1953; a 62-3 romp past N.C. State in 1993, a game in which quarterback Charlie Ward broke Gary Huff's total career yardage; 73-14 against Tulane in 1987; 72-13 versus Wake Forest in 1995; and 59-0 over South Carolina in 1988.

In that last game, the Gamecock fans behind the FSU bench heckled the visitors pretty badly in the early going, especially Deion Sanders. Prime Time had the last laugh, though, "standing on the bench late in the game, back to the field, and urging the Gamecocks' fans to go and demand their money back after witnessing such a lame performance."

The tenth greatest margin of victory in FSU history is 58 points, which came in a 58-0 romp over Western Michigan in 1991.

For FSU fans, this is indeed a list of ten to remember for the ages.

You've got your list and you're ready to go: a gallon of paint and a water hose from the hardware store; chips, peanuts, and sodas from the grocery store for watching tonight's football game on TV with your buddies; the tickets for the band concert; the clothes from the dry cleaners. You have so many errands to run that you need a list to make sure you get them all done.

God himself once made a list of things he wanted us all never to forget, assigning to Moses the secretarial duties. We have come to call God's list the Ten Commandments.

Just as your list reminds you to do something, so does God's list remind you of how you are to act in your dealings with other people and with him. A life dedicated to Jesus is a life devoted to relationships, and God's list emphasizes that the social life and the spiritual life of the faithful cannot be sundered. God's relationship to you is one of unceasing and unqualified love, and you are to mirror that divine love in your relationships with others.

In case you forget, you have a list.

Do you really mind me quoting the Ten Commandments to your sons?
-- Bobby Bowden

God's list is a set of instructions on how you are to conduct yourself with other people and with him.

DAY 78

REGRETS, ANYONE?

Read 2 Corinthians 7:8-13.

"Godly sorrow brings repentance that leads to salvation and leaves no regret" (v. 10).

I wouldn't do that any differently." Like most coaches, that's what Bobby Bowden said about decisions his staff and he made during games. In his career of more than fifty years, however, there was one notable exception.

The Miami game of 1987 was one of those legendary titanic battles so common to the series, this one between the teams that would finish one-two in the national rankings. With 42 seconds left to play, Ronald Lewis caught an 18-yard touchdown pass from Danny McManus to pull FSU to within one at 26-25. In this day before overtime, Bowden elected to go for the win. A pass was knocked down and Miami won, the Seminoles' only loss.

"Right now I would kick," Bowden said years later. "Back in those days, I had never gone for a tie, and I let that get the best of me. . . . It was just a macho kind of thing."

In the locker room after the game, Bowden apologized to his players and told them they should have kicked. "I felt like I had let them down," Bowden said.

Tight end Pat Carter, for whom the conversion pass was intended, was among the many players who would have none of it. "I felt that wasn't necessary," he said about Bowden's apology. Tailback Sammie Smith, a first-round draft pick by the Miami

SEMINOLES

Dolphins, agreed, explaining that during the timeout as the decision was discussed, he and Deion Sanders both urged the coaches to go for two.

Bowden admitted the players' sentiment made him feel a little better. Still . . .

In their hit "The Class of '57," the legendary Statler Brothers served up some pure country truth when they sang, "Things get complicated when you get past 18." That complication includes regrets; you have them; so does everyone else: relationships and situations that upon reflection we wish we had handled differently.

Feeling troubled or remorseful over something you've done or left undone is not necessarily a bad thing. That's because God uses regrets to spur us to repentance, which is the decision to change our ways. Repentance in turn is essential to salvation through Jesus Christ. You regret your un-Christlike actions, you repent by promising God to mend your ways, and then you seek and receive forgiveness for them.

The cold, hard truth is that no matter how many regrets you have now, you will have more in your life along the way. You can know absolutely, however, that you will never, ever regret making Jesus the reason for that life.

The only regret I have is that I never had a chance to play for Bobby Bowden.
-- Burt Reynolds

**Regrets are part of living,
but you'll never regret living for Jesus.**

DAY 79

FAME

Read 1 Kings 10:1-10, 18-29.

"King Solomon was greater in riches and wisdom than all the other kings of the earth. The whole world sought audience with Solomon" (vv. 23-24).

They should be among the most famous athletes in FSU history, but they aren't. They are Lisa Young (Walters), Jane Geddes, Barbara Bunkowsky (Scherbak), Marla Anderson, and Michelle Guibault. Their claim to fame? They won a national championship at FSU.

They were the five aces of the 1981 FSU women's golf team, and they remain to this day one of the greatest assemblages of talent in Seminole history. One rival coach told FSU coach Verlyn Giles that "watching the team get off the van was like watching an NFL team get out, four linemen and a place-kicker." Anderson was the place-kicker, surrounded by four power players, three of whom went on to the LPGA.

The golf national championship was played in Athens, and after two rounds, the Noles trailed Georgia by eight strokes. They made their move the third day with Young shooting a 71. FSU took a one-stroke lead into the final round, which was a two-team slugfest. Georgia regained the lead by a stroke at the turn. Then came the par-5 seventeenth. "We made mincemeat of the par-fives," team member Debbie Dillman said. (Dillman went on to become a legendary golf coach at FSU.) "That one hole absolutely won it for us."

The Noles made four birdies on the hole, and the national championship was theirs by three strokes over Georgia.

The great misfortune of that 1981 team was that the players won the last national title of the defunct AIAW. They never even received championship rings from the athletic department.

Have you ever wanted to be famous? Hanging out with other rich and famous people, having people listen to what you say, throwing money around like toilet paper, meeting adoring and clamoring fans, and posing for the paparazzi?

Fame is alluring and dangerous. The story of the movie or rock star who finds fame and then plunges into alcohol- or drug-induced misery is apocryphal. That's because fame can easily become an idol into which people place their hopes for satisfaction and meaning in their life.

Being famous basically means your name and your face are well known. The truth is you are already quite famous because God knows your name, your face, and everything about you. If a photographer snapped you pondering this fame – the only kind that can make life worthwhile – would the picture show the world unbridled joy or the shell-shocked expression of a mug shot?

When you play a sport, you have two things in mind. One is to get into the Hall of Fame and the other is to go to heaven when you die.

– Lee Trevino

**You're already quite famous because God knows
your name and your face, which you may find
either reassuring or terrifying.**

DAY 80

A LONG SHOT

Read Matthew 9:9-13.

"[Jesus] saw a man named Matthew sitting at the tax collector's booth. 'Follow me,' he told him, and Matthew got up and followed him" (v. 9).

Clifton Abraham was a long shot.

Abraham was an All-American cornerback (1994) who started three years for the Noles, including the 1993 national championship season. He was twice All-ACC, set a school record with four touchdowns off blocked kicks, and went on to play three seasons in the NFL. He was small, only 5-9, but he once said, "People who might think I'm too small don't know what's inside of me."

Abraham grew up in a tough section of Dallas. At a party in high school, he bent over to pick up his hat, no more than an arm's length from a friend, Quincy Green. "That's when I heard, 'Pow! Pow! Pow! Pow!'" Abraham said. Bullets were flying from a drive-by shooting. Green fell, and Abraham recalled he started laughing. "We were like, 'Man, I thought you were in shape.'" But Green had been shot and he died.

"A lot of crime," Abraham said about his neighborhood. "Everybody's into drugs and sex and everything else." His twin brothers were imprisoned after felony convictions. In May 1989, because a girlfriend complained he wasn't spending enough time with her, he rejected an invitation to hang out with some friends. They

SEMINOLES

robbed a store and got caught; five were football teammates and they went to prison. Abraham knew that had he been there, peer pressure would have made it too easy to go along.

But Clifton Abraham, the long shot who knew he was his momma's "last hope," battled the odds and made it out.

Matthew the tax collector was another long shot, an unlikely person to be a confidant of the Son of God. While we may not get all warm and fuzzy about the IRS, our government's revenue agents are nothing like Matthew and his ilk. He basically bought a franchise, paying the Roman Empire for the privilege of extorting, bullying, and stealing everything he could from his own people. John MacArthur described tax collectors of the time as "despicable, vile, unprincipled scoundrels."

And yet, Jesus said only two words to this lowlife: "Follow me." With divine insight, Jesus knew that this long shot would make an excellent disciple.

It's the same with us. While we may not be quite as vile as Matthew was, none of us can stand before God with our hands clean and our hearts pure. We are all impossibly long shots to enter God's Heaven. That is, until we do what Matthew did: get up and follow Jesus.

Football is a way to help [Clifton] get what he wants – a better life, a better environment – than what he was raised in.
-- FSU defensive coordinator Mickey Andrews

**Only through Jesus does our status change
from being long shots to enter God's kingdom
to being heavy favorites.**

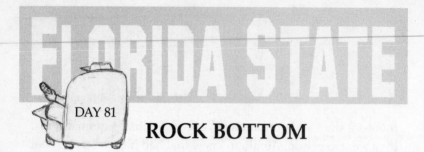

DAY 81

ROCK BOTTOM

Read Psalm 23.

*"Even though I walk through the valley of the shadow
of death, I will fear no evil for you are with me; your rod
and your staff, they comfort me" (v. 4).*

When Darrell Mudra took over as the FSU head football coach
in 1974, the Seminole program had hit rock bottom.

Mudra has been referred to as the "Rodney Dangerfield of FSU
coaches," perhaps best remembered by Nole fans for coaching
games from the press box and not the sidelines. The Seminole
faithful are probably are aware, too, that Mudra's record in Tallahassee was a miserable 4-18-0. Only a perceptive fan might understand, however, that the cold, hard numbers don't reveal how far
down rock bottom for FSU was. The Noles were 0-11 in 1973, and
they weren't very competitive. They lost to Kansas 28-0, Miss.
State 37-12, San Diego State 38-17, Houston 34-3, Virginia Tech
36-13, South Carolina 52-12, and Florida 49-0.

That's what Mudra inherited, and the mess wasn't just on the
field. There was no weight room, for instance. Mudra had a coach
locate some used Nautilus machines to begin the Seminole weight
program.

Mudra's players were all over the place. They lived in Cash Hall,
which Mudra called "a den of iniquity," studied in the history
building, and ate in the Student Union. The athletic department
bought a motel to solve the housing problem. Mudra took money

designated for offices and used it to build a weight room and an area where the players could study and eat together.

Mudra's two teams went 1-10 in 1974 and 3-8 in 1975; he was gone and Bobby Bowden was in. Bowden knew, though, how bad it had been and what Mudra had done. He once told Mudra and his players that the 1975 team had really turned the program around, had rescued it from rock bottom.

Maybe it was the day your business went under, taking everything you owned with it. Or the night your spouse walked out. Or the afternoon you learned your child was seriously, perhaps deathly, ill. You've known rock bottom.

Rock bottom is the time when life is its darkest, when you "walk through the valley of the shadow of death." You are down in a dark valley looking up at the mountain peaks where the sun shines and people laugh and have hope. Rock bottom is the time when life is its loneliest, when "friends" and acquaintances desert you and the train wreck that is your life.

And yet in that darkness and that loneliness, you will find your best friend. You will find Jesus, who's been in that valley ahead of you. He knows sorrow, suffering, loss, and pain. Trust in him and he'll take you where he wound up after he walked through that valley; he'll take you all the way to glory.

We took over a program that was really in disarray.
— *Coach Darrell Mudra*

**"Nobody knows what I'm going through!";
Jesus does because he's been there.**

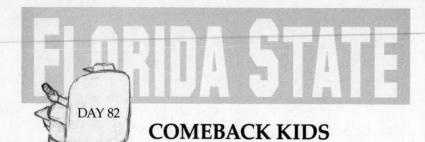

COMEBACK KIDS

Read Acts 9:1-22

*"All those who heard him were astonished and asked,
'Isn't he the man who raised havoc in Jerusalem among
those who call on this name?'" (v. 21)*

If you left the Civic Center early on Jan. 22, 2004, you're forgiven
– but you missed one of the greatest comebacks in Florida State
sports history.

A packed house of Seminole fans was disappointed and disap-
proving as the North Carolina Tar Heels all but blew FSU out
of its own gymnasium in the first half. At one point, the Heels
scored 21 straight points to lead 42-18.

But Seminole Coach Leonard Hamilton knew his team hadn't
quit, and UNC Coach Roy Williams also knew the game wasn't
over despite the huge lead late in the first half. "It was fool's gold
early in the game," he said. "Everybody was thinking it was going
to be easy."

The Noles showed some life and some pluck by closing the
half with a flourish, outscoring Carolina 17-7 to cut the margin
to 49-35 at the break. And then Tim Pickett found his shot. He
poured in 20 points the last half, finishing the night with 30. FSU
kept creeping closer, and closer, and closer until sophomore point
guard Todd Galloway nailed a three at the buzzer to send the
game into overtime and the crowd into delirium.

When FSU's defense forced UNC to miss its first seven shots in

SEMINOLES

overtime, the Noles took control of the game. They won 90-81 to complete an incredible 33-point turnaround.

Hamilton said he couldn't recall any team he'd been involved with that had ever come from as many as 24 points down to win a game, especially against a team as talented as the Tar Heels.

The team finished the season 19-14, and for one marvelous night, they pulled off a comeback for the ages.

Life will have its setbacks whether they result from personal failures or from forces and people beyond your control. Being a Christian and a faithful follower of Jesus Christ doesn't insulate you from getting into deep trouble. Maybe financial problems suffocated you. A serious illness put you on the sidelines. Or your family was hit with a great tragedy. Life is a series of victories and defeats. Winning isn't about avoiding defeat; it's about getting back up to compete again. It's about making a comeback of your own.

When you avail yourself of God's grace and God's power, your comeback is always greater than your setback. You are never too far behind, and it's never too late in life's game for Jesus to lead you to victory, to turn trouble into triumph.

As it was with the Seminoles against North Carolina for one night and with Paul in his entire life, it's not how you start that counts; it's how you finish.

Turn a setback into a comeback.

--Football coach Billy Brewer

**In life, victory is truly a matter of how you finish
and whether you finish with Jesus at your side.**

DAY 83

CAN'T GO WRONG

Read Galatians 6:7-10.

"Let us not grow weary in doing what is right, for we will reap at harvest time, if we do not give up" (v. 9 NRSV).

Coach Mike Martin did the right thing for FSU even though for a while it looked as though he had ripped the heart out of his team.

Martin's 1994 baseball team was in the middle of a home series against Duke when he took the unprecedented step of kicking four players off the team, including the squad's starting center-fielder. Their transgression? They all planned to transfer. Despite some misgivings, Martin had originally approved their staying on the team until the end of the season, but something happened in that Duke series that gained him a new perspective and led him to change his mind and take his drastic action.

With the Seminoles in a mild slump, having lost three of their last four, Martin hoped to lift his team's spirits by showing them a motivational video. When the tape was over, one of the exiting players strolled into Martin's office and asked the coach if he could do anything to speed up the transfer. "That stunned me," Martin said. "I asked myself, 'Could I send somebody out there who didn't have his heart and soul into playing for Florida State? I knew then that I had to have them leave. All of them."

So he gave the four players the boot. And that shake-up revitalized the team and set the Noles off on a winning streak, right?

Not exactly. The team promptly lost four of its next six games, but Martin never doubted what he had done. "The decision had to be one of the most difficult, painful decisions I've ever had to make," he said. "But I had to do what was the right thing for Florida State University."

The team ultimately righted itself, making it all the way to the college world series and finishing with a 53-22 record and a No. 6 national ranking.

Doing the right thing is easy when it's little stuff. Giving the quarter back when the cashier gives you too much change, helping a lost child at the mall, or putting a few bucks in the honor box at your favorite fishing hole.

But what about when it costs you? Every day you have many chances to do the right thing; each time, you have a choice: right or wrong. The factors that weigh into your decisions – including the personal cost to you – reveal much about your character.

Does your doing the right thing ever depend upon your calculation of the odds of getting caught? In the world's eyes, you can't go wrong doing wrong when you won't get caught. That may pass as the world's slippery situational ethics, but it doesn't pass muster with God.

In God's eyes, you can't go wrong doing right. Ever.

I won't tolerate a womanizer, I won't tolerate a drunk, and I won't tolerate a cheater. Those are the things that'll cost you your job.
--Bobby Bowden to his assistant coaches

As far as God is concerned, you can never go wrong doing right.

HOME IMPROVEMENT

Read Hebrews 6:1-12.

"Let us go on towards perfection" (v. 1 NRSV).

FSU's first three football teams had no stadium to call their own, but just look where the Seminoles frolic now!

On Oct. 18, 1947, Don Grant returned a Stetson kickoff to the FSU 32 while 7,165 fans watched at old Centennial Field. Florida State football had begun.

It wasn't until 1950, however, that the Seminoles had a home stadium. The first game was played at Doak S. Campbell Stadium on Oct. 7, 1950, against Randolph-Macon. FSU won 40-7 before 9,676 fans.

Doak Campbell Stadium was built on an old cow pasture and was completed in only five months at a cost of $250,000. Its original capacity was 15,000. Tallahasseean Rainey Cawthon sold more than 1,000 season tickets at $50 each to help fund the stadium. He won a wheelbarrow ride down Monroe Street from the stadium's contractor, Red Coleman. During the summer, FSU football players painted the stadium; they were paid $1 an hour for their work.

Throughout its history, Doak Campbell Stadium has constantly been upgraded and improved. Nine expansions over the years ultimately increased the stadium's capacity to more than 82,000. The south end zone got its own video board for the 2008 season. A new sound system was installed in 2007. A new playing surface was installed in 2004. It required excavating the stadium's floor eight inches deep, removing the old drainage system, and installing a system built to professional-course golf green standards. Skyboxes now tower above the action on Bobby Bowden Field.

Great as it is, Doak Campbell Stadium will always be subject to renovation to improve it. The same is true for our lives; they can always stand some improvement.

It's not just the "New Year's Resolutions" improvements we need to make either. You know the kind: lose weight, be more punctual, spend more time with the kids. More important than those are the spiritual improvements we should be constantly making.

You can always know more about God's word, discover more ways to serve God, deepen your prayer life and your trust in God, and do a better job of being Jesus to other people through simple acts of kindness and caring.

You are always "under construction" as far as God is concerned because you are always striving toward spiritual perfection. Build constantly until the day you stand before God with all of your work done. You will present him a finished product, and you will want it to be a spiritual mansion, not a hovel.

The principle is competing against yourself. It's about self-improvement, about being better than you were the day before.
— Former NFL quarterback Steve Young

**Renovation and sprucing up should be ongoing
for your body and your soul.**

DAY 85

IN GOD'S OWN TIME

Read Colossians 3:12-17.

"Therefore, as God's chosen people, holy and dearly loved, clothe yourselves with compassion, kindness, humility, gentleness and patience" (v. 12).

The game was over, but Bobby Bowden still had to wait to see if the Seminoles and he had finally won a national championship.

The 18-16 win over Nebraska in the 1994 Orange Bowl seemed to wrap up the title for FSU, which sportswriter John Nogowski said Bowden had pursued "like a man chasing a mirage in the desert." But the final say lay with the polls, and strong sentiment existed for Notre Dame, which had handed the Seminoles their only loss.

Bowden had it all figured out, he hoped. "We were number three (in the CNN/*USA Today* poll), Notre Dame was number four, and we beat number one," Bowden said. "How are they going to throw Notre Dame up ahead of us?"

They didn't. The pollsters voted the Seminoles number one, thus securing the lone team achievement that had eluded Bowden in his glorious career.

Time after time his teams came so close. Bowden once said he wasn't losing any sleep over not winning a national title, but he finally took to joking about it, undoubtedly to ease some of the disappointment. As Nogowski put it, the Seminoles "have seemed cursed in big games with a mind-bending facility for snatching defeat from the jaws of victory." A lesser program might have been devastated by such losses, but the Noles kept coming back until the title was theirs.

Bowden's patience may have been tested, but he never wavered in his belief that FSU would win a national championship. After years of waiting, he was rewarded. Twice in fact. (See 1999.)

Have you ever left a restaurant because the server didn't take your order quickly enough? Complained at your doctor's office about how long you had to wait? Wondered how much longer a sermon was going to last?

It isn't just the machinations of the world with which we're impatient; we want God to move at our pace, not his. For instance, how often have you prayed and expected – indeed, demanded – an immediate answer from God? And aren't Christians the world over impatient for the glorious day when Jesus will return and set everything right? We're in a hurry but God obviously isn't.

As rare as it seems to be, patience is nevertheless included among the likes of gentleness, humility, kindness, and compassion as attributes of a Christian.

God expects us to be patient. He knows what he's doing, he is in control, and his will shall be done. On his schedule, not ours.

After getting so close . . ., I was beginning to wonder if I would ever get to come here.

> -- *Bobby Bowden at the White House after winning the 1993 national title*

God moves in his own time, so often we must wait for him to act, remaining faithful and hopeful.

CHANGELESS

Read Hebrews 13:5-16.

"Jesus Christ is the same yesterday and today and forever" (v. 8).

What game is this?

The helmet was a piece of leather with cotton under it, so the players let their hair grow long for additional protection. The ball was the shape of a watermelon, too big to hold in your hand and pass. A nose guard was about the only protection a player had. A player might have shoulder pads and hip pads, but only if he provided them himself.

Hiding the ball under a jersey. A field-goal kicker using his helmet for a tee. Spectators rushing onto the field and getting in the players' way. Players dragging ball carriers forward. Linemen holding hands and jumping to the right or to the left just before a play began. Darkness forcing games to be called. Teams deciding upon the length of the game once they showed up.

What game is this?

This was the wild and wooly game of college football in its early days, the 1890s and the turn of the century. Only a year after West Florida Seminary became Florida State College in 1901, the school fielded its first football team. Largely unregulated and unsophisticated with no forward pass, it was a game we would barely recognize today.

Thank goodness, we might well say. Given the symmetry, the

excitement, the passion, and the sheer spectacle that surround today's college game, few, if any, FSU fans would long for the days when handles were sewn into the uniforms of ball carriers to make them easier to toss.

Football has changed – but then again so has everything else. Computers and CDs, cell phones and George Foreman grills – they may not have even been around when you were sixteen. Think about how style, cars, and tax laws constantly change. Don't be too harsh on the world, though, because you've changed also. You've aged, gained or lost weight, gotten married, changed jobs, or relocated.

Have you ever found yourself bewildered by the rapid pace of change, casting about for something to hold on to that will always be the same, that you can use as an anchor for your life? Is there anything like that in this world?

Sadly, the answer is no. As football illustrates, all the things of this world change.

On the other hand, there's Jesus, who is the same today, the same forever, always dependable, always loving you. You can grab hold of Jesus and never let go.

Baseball is for the leisurely afternoons of summer and for the unchanging dreams.
-- Writer Roger Kahn

In our ever-changing and bewildering world,
Jesus is the same forever;
his love for you will never change.

CONFIDENCE MAN

Read Micah 7:5-7.

"As for me, I will look to the Lord, I will wait for the God of my salvation" (v. 7 NRSV).

Peter Warrick was such a supremely confident football player that in the national championship game against Virginia Tech on Jan. 4, 2000, he called his own shot, the one that finished off the Hokies.

A wide receiver, Warrick was All-ACC three times (1997-99) and All-America in 1998 and '99. His senior season was marred by a monumental lapse in judgment when a teammate and he accepted some designer clothing from Dillard's department store for pocket change. A contrite Warrick expressed a desire before the Sugar Bowl showdown with Tech to do something that would make fans "remember me for what I did on the field, not how I messed up off the field."

FSU led 39-29 in the fourth quarter when Warrick trotted into the huddle and turned to his offensive linemen. "What do y'all want me to do?" he asked. "Y'all want me to finish 'em?" Guard Jason Whitaker later verified Warrick's question and the linemen's response: "Finish 'em, Pete." And so Warrick did.

Sports writer Gary Long described Chris Weinke's subsequent heave and Warrick's catch: With a Tech defender sprinting step for step with him toward the goal line, "Warrick's left hand tipped the ball, and as he was falling onto his left side away from the defender, he freed his arms to momentarily juggle and then secure the ball to his body." The spectacular touchdown catch was Warrick's third score of the night.

FSU had a 46-29 win and the national title, and a confident Peter Warrick was named the game's MVP.

You both need and demonstrate confidence in all areas of your life. You're confident, for instance, that the company you work for will pay you on time, or you wouldn't go to work. You turn the ignition confident your car will start. When you flip a switch, you expect the light to come on. The foundation of your marriage is your confidence in your spouse's faithfulness.

But the tragic truth is that confidence placed in the people and the things of this world is confidence misplaced. Companies go broke; car batteries die; light bulbs burn out; people lie and cheat. Life often seems very determined to shatter our confidence.

So where does that leave you? Where can you place your trust with absolute confidence that you won't be betrayed? In the One True God. The Bible is a record of God's dealings with his creation, and the story it tells is one of God's fidelity. God says what he means and does what he says he will. You can count on God – always.

When it gets right down to the wood-chopping, the key to winning is confidence.

-- Coach Darrell Royal

People, things, and organizations will let you down; only God can be trusted absolutely and confidently.

DAY 88

PLAYING WITH PAIN

Read 2 Corinthians 1:3-7.

*"Just as the sufferings of Christ flow over into our lives,
so also through Christ our comfort overflows" (v. 5).*

Everything is routine, except for the pain. I'll never get used to the pain."

So spoke Arleshia Davidson, a 6-2 center-forward for the Seminoles, as her junior season of 1997-98 got under way.

Davidson received "a second look virtually every time she stepped onto a basketball court" because of "what appeared to be a fashion statement: socks pulled up to the knees covering three layers of tape. 'A lot of people laugh,' Davidson said. 'I'm like, 'If only you knew.'"

What those who laughed so carelessly at Davidson's attire didn't know was that she should never have been playing basketball in the first place. The tape and those socks that drew chortles and snickers secured padding that protected at least five stress fractures on each of Davidson's shins. The pain could be treated, not cured, so Davidson took painkillers every day and wore a bone-stimulating coil around both shins for eight hours every night.

What did the pain feel like? Davidson called it "excruciating, like somebody's gnawing at my leg with an ice pick." Coach Sue Semrau said, "Most people stop playing if there's one line on each shin." And Davidson had five or six. On each shin.

So why do it? Davidson preferred life in constant pain to life without basketball. "I love the game. It's that simple," she said. With her status in doubt for every game, she prayed at night, "Please God, don't let the doctor tell me I can't play basketball again."

And the doctor didn't – and Arleshia Davidson played with the pain, which did, however, eventually force her to have steel rods placed in both legs before her senior season. Even that didn't stop her from playing on.

Since you live on Earth and not in Heaven, you are forced to play with pain. Whether it's a car wreck that left you shattered, the end of a relationship that left you battered, or a loved one's death that left you tattered -- pain finds you and challenges you to keep going.

While God's word teaches that you will reap what you sow, life also teaches that pain and hardship are not necessarily the result of personal failure. Pain in fact can be one of the tools God uses to mold your character and change your life.

What are you to do when you are hit full-speed by the awful pain that seems to choke the very will to live out of you? Where is your consolation, your comfort, and your help?

In almighty God, whose love will never fail. When life knocks you to your knees, you're closer to God than ever before.

It hurts up to a point and then it doesn't get any worse.
-- Ultramarathon runner Ann Trason

**When life hits you with pain, turn to God
for comfort, consolation, and hope.**

DAY 89

AT A LOSS

Read Philippians 3:7-11.

"I consider everything a loss compared to the surpassing greatness of knowing Christ Jesus my Lord, for whose sake I have lost all things" (v. 8).

His grandfather. His sister. His mother. When he was 11, Marvin Jones lost them all within the space of three months.

As a junior in 1992, Jones became the first Florida State player in history to win two national awards the same year when he won the Butkus and Lombardi awards as the nation's top linebacker and lineman respectively. He was a two-time All-America who was drafted in the first round by the New York Jets after his junior season. He enjoyed an All-Pro career and is a member of the FSU Hall of Fame.

Jones' reputation at FSU was as a hitter. "When he hits people, he means it," sportswriter Sally Jenkins said. Adept with a phrase, Jones said he ate running backs "with ketchup. It takes the bad taste away." He once described the perfect hit as "when I achieve total blackness. Oh, it's lovely."

Despite all that ferocity, a prerequisite for an All-American-caliber linebacker, Jones nevertheless, Jenkins wrote, retained a "little-boy-lost quality." That's because of the staggering series of losses Jones experienced from November 1983 through February 1984.

His paternal grandfather died in the middle of November. On

Dec. 21, his sister, 23-year-old Barbara, died after years of heart problems. Then Jones' mother died of heart failure on Feb. 14. "It got so we were afraid to pick up the phone," Jones said.

In remembering his mother, Jones said, "The thing about it is, I never told her how much I loved her. I was young. I didn't have a talkative relationship."

Sometime in your youth or early adult life, you learned that loss is a part of life. Maybe, as it was with Marvin Jones, it was when a family member died. Perhaps it wasn't so devastatingly tragic: your puppy died, your best friend moved away, or an older sibling left home.

Loss inevitably diminishes your life, but loss and the grief that accompanies it are an inevitable part of the price of loving. When you first encountered loss, you learned that you were virtually helpless to prevent it or escape it.

There is life after loss, though, because you have one sure place to turn. Jesus can share your pain and ease your suffering, but he doesn't stop there. Through the loss of his own life, he has transformed death -- the ultimate loss -- into the ultimate gain of eternal life. In Jesus lies the promise that one day loss itself will be the big loser.

To win, you have to risk loss.

-- Olympic champion skier Jean-Claude Killy

Jesus not only eases the pain of our losses but transforms the loss caused by death into the gain of eternal life, thereby defeating loss forever.

DAY 90

CROWD CONTROL

Read Matthew 27:15-26.

"When Pilate saw that he could do nothing, but rather that a riot was beginning, he took some water and washed his hands before the crowd" (v. 24 NRSV).

Bobby Bowden never wanted "yes" men on his staff. He certainly didn't get one when he hired Wayne McDuffie.

"I don't like 'yes' men," Bowden said once. "'Yes' men bother me more than anything else 'cause you might want to do some strategy that is wrong, and if they agree with you just because you are the boss, you get yourself beat."

McDuffie was Bowden's offensive coordinator from 1983 through 1989. Bowden called him the "most controversial" guy he ever worked with and "a tough nut, but I loved him." The two frequently had confrontations behind closed doors. That's because McDuffie was "the most demonstrative of any of Bowden's offensive coordinators when it came to objecting to Bowden's play calling."

More than once, McDuffie left the press box in a huff while the game was still going on. Once he even got involved in a car wreck -- and the Noles were still playing.

Then the tight ends coach, Brad Scott remembered Bowden's calling for McDuffie, who would be gone, often out of frustration because a play he had called never made it to the field. "The only thing I could think to say was that he was in the bathroom," Scott

SEMINOLES

recalled. "That was kind of the standard answer."

During the 1985 Auburn game, Bowden repeatedly harangued McDuffie to get the offense in a fourth-and-one situation so they could run a trick play he felt would score. Finally, McDuffie said to his boss in exasperation, "We don't have a dadgum call to get it in fourth and one."

Wayne McDuffie was not a "yes" man; he never just went along with the crowd, not even when it was his legendary boss.

Teenagers seem to catch particular grief about going along with the crowd, but adults, too, often behave in ways contrary to what their conscience tells them is right simply because they fear the disapproval of the people they're with at the time.

So they chuckle at a racial joke. Make fun of a coworker nobody likes. Drink too much and stay out too late. Remain silent when God is cursed.

It remains true, though: Just because the crowd does it doesn't make it right. Even Pontius Pilate understood that.

The followers of Jesus Christ are called to separate themselves from the crowd by being disciples. That is, we give to Jesus nothing less than everything we are and everything we have. Jesus is the top priority in a disciple's life, and everything else – everything else – stands behind Jesus.

A disciple never goes along with the crowd; he goes along with Jesus.

Never compromise what you think is right.

-- *Bear Bryant*

A disciple of Jesus follows him, not the crowd.

NOTES
(by Devotion Day Number)

1   They played for three seasons, wearing purple and gold.: *Seminole Football: 2007 Florida State Media Guide*, p. 204, www.seminoles.com.

1   "with the G.I. Bill . . . Florida State University in 1947.: Philip L. Ben, *Seminole Gold* (Marietta, GA: Longstreet Press, Inc., 1996), p. 52.

1   The first FSU football team . . . from the ranks of the student body.: Ben, p. 55.

2   conditions that required ball boys . . . running from the beams.: Mary Ann Lindley, "We Almost Saw a Basketball Game Get Rained Out," *Tallahassee Democrat*, Dec. 1, 1994, p. 1B, http://infoweb.newsbank.com/iw-search/we/InfoWeb?p_action=doc&p_docid=0Eb598D7, July 23, 2008.

3   Nicknamed "Jingle Joints" . . . fly off in different directions,: Pat Putnam, "Jingle Joints Should Be Judged by His Cover," *Sports Illustrated*, Sept. 30, 1968, http://vault.sportsillustrated.cnn.com/vault/article/magazine/MAG1081639/index.htm, July 14, 2008.

3   In 1967, Florida coach . . . never did sign that original.: Putnam.

4   "He's unreal. . . . player in the world.": Gary Long, *Stadium Stories: Florida State Seminoles* (Guilford, CN: The Globe Pequot Press, 2006), p. 141.

4   "If he weighed 215 pounds, he'd be illegal.": Long, p. 184.

4   the team already had . . . where we'll play you.": Bobby Bowden with Steve Ellis, *Bobby Bowden's Tales from the Seminoles Sideline* (Champaign, IL: Sports Publishing L.L.C., 2004), pp. 112-13.

4   in the preseason, injuries . . . the ball under his arm.": Bowden with Ellis, pp. 113-14.

4   I've always asked for . . . I definitely believe in prayer.: Jim and Julie S. Bettinger, *The Book of Bowden* (Nashville: TowleHouse Publishing, 2001), p. 95.

5   For years Bobby Bowden kept an empty picture frame in his office.: "A Brief History of Florida State Football," *Seminole Football: 2007 Florida State Media Guide*, p. 204.

5   I think many Christians make a mistake. Nobody's perfect.: Bettinger, p. 21.

6   "I think that 10-0 win . . . Georgia, Miami, and Georgia Tech.: Long, p. 70.

6   FSU coach Tom Nugent conducted . . . . We just teach great football.": Long, p. 71.

6   "monumental" and "earthshaking." . . . legitimacy in the South.": Long, p. 71.

6   I am living proof that . . . do unbelievable things.: Bettinger, p. 67.

7   Shortstop Darby Cottle and second . . . hit .477 for the season.: "1981 & 1982 National Champions," *Florida State University: 2008 Seminole Softball*, p. 69, www.seminoles.com.

7   their 8-6 edge in the series . . . Toni Robinette, and Sikes.: "1981 & 1982 National Champions."

7   "the players on those . . . legacy that continues today.": :1981 & 1982 National Champions."

7   "We do not choose whether . . . on which we will stand.": R. Alan Culpepper, "The Gospel of Luke: Introduction, Commentary, and Reflections,"

The New Interpreter's Bible (Nashville: Abingdon Press, 1995), Vol. IX, p. 153.

8 College football analyst Beano . . . *My Fair Lady*.": Long, p. 163.

8 "'Puntrooskie' will forever reign . . . football teams have attempted.": Long, p. 164.

8 The tenth-ranked Noles . . . with only 1:33 left to play.: Long, p. 164.

8 center David Willingham snapped . . . to the Clemson one.: Long, pp. 165-66.

8 When you run trick plays . . . folks question your sanity.: Bettinger, p. 32.

9 In the third game of . . . wish they'd admit it.": Long, p. 81.

9 one former Gator student . . . at the time, Lawton Chiles.: Long, pp. 81-2.

9 Wetherell said he had . . . cost him 100,000 votes.": Long, pp. 82-3.

9 None of us wants justice . . . we'd all go to hell.: Bettinger, p. 69.

10 On Jan. 21, 1991, Bowden wrote . . . and quarterback the Seminoles.: Bowden with Ellis, pp. 115-16.

10 "I never expected to hear . . . wants to come back.": Bowden with Ellis, p. 116.

10 The immediate concern was whether . . . even if it cost them Henson.: Bowden with Ellis, p. 117.

10 "I made a promise to you . . . we'd love to have you back.": Bowden with Ellis, p. 119.

11 "rivals the 100 points . . . right behind the infield.": Mark Bechtel, "Heavy Metal Rap," *Sports Illustrated*, March 13, 2000, http://vault.sportsillustrated.ccn.com/vault/article/magazine/MAG1018533/index.htm, July 14, 2008.

11 McDougall was told repeatedly . . . This guy's special.": Bechtel.

12 "the most spectacular tradition in all of college football.": *Seminole Football: 2007 Florida State Media Guide*, p. 207.

12 "You're starting the fire . . . he's ready to charge.": Melanie Yeager, "The Most Wonderful Tradition,'" *Tallahassee Democrat*, Nov. 16, 2002, p. B1, http://infoweb.newsbank.com/iw-search/we/InfoWeb?p_action=doc&p_docid=0Fb36F15, July 23, 2008.

12 The tradition was born on Sept. 16, 1978, against Oklahoma State.: *Seminole Football: 2007 Florida State Media Guide*, p. 207.

12 The idea was the brainstorm . . . of the Seminole Indians,": Yeager.

12 Chief Osceola and Renegade are the most wonderful tradition in college football.: Yeager.

13 "We had the game won," . . . to be on top of it,": Bowden with Ellis, pp. 151-52.

14 He had a six-year, . . . Dix wanted to graduate.: "Walter Dix Profile & Bio," *2008 Beijing Summer Olympics*, http://www.nbcolympics.com/athletes/athlete=158/bio/index.html, Aug. 25, 2008.

14 "I don't care about signing . . . in that garnet and gold uniform.: Corey Clark, "Loyalty Lets FSU Track Star Dix Cash In," *Tallahassee Democrat*, July 10, 2008, http://nolesports.tallahassee.com/apps/pbcs.dll/article?AID=/20080710/FSU09/807100336, July 19, 2008.

14 Shortly after his performance . . . to be for seven figures.: "Walter Dix Profile & Bio."

15 "the stadium seated 41,000 and we were averaging 17,000 fans per game.": Mark Schlabach, *What It Means to Be a Seminole*, (Chicago: Triumph Brooks, 2007), p. v.

15   He scheduled some of the nation's . . . can survive that thing.": Rick Reilly, "The Road to Victory," *Sports Illustrated*, Sept. 5, 1988, http://vault.sportsillustrated.cnn.com/vault/article/magazine/MAG1067720/2/index.htm, July 14, 2008.

15   a game Bowden said drew national attention to Florida State,: Schlabach, p. v.

16   Ed Jonas, one of . . . win a varsity letter at FSU.: Gerald Ensley, "Show of 'Sportsmanship' Endures," *Tallahassee Democrat*, Dec. 4, 2000, p. B1, http://infoweb.newsbank.com/iw-search/we/InfoWeb?p_action=doc&p_docid=0EB5985B, July 23, 2008.

17   The coaches introduced an offensive package . . . called in the game.: Bowden with Ellis, pp. 87-8.

18   Ken Alexander and Alonzo Horner . . . yells and helmet pounding." Tim Layden, "Heart and Soul," *Sports Illustrated*, Dec. 30, 1996, http://vault.sportsillustrated.cnn.com/vault/article/magazine/MAG1009291/2/index.htm, July 14, 2008.

18   In the Noles' 34-16 win . . . athletes of past decades." Layden, "Heart and Soul."

18   I tell my players," . . . same ingredients in each of us.": Bettinger, p. 123.

19   When she was at FSU, . . . *Elle* magazine said so. "Gabrielle Reece," *Wikipedia, the free encyclopedia*, http://en.wikipedia.org/wiki/Gabrielle_Reece, Aug. 11, 2008.

19   "arguably the most famous female athlete of all.": Mark Fitzhenry, "Reece Shares Her Life as a 'Big Girl,'" *Tallahassee Democrat*, July 27, 1997, p. 1E, http://infoweb.newsbank.com/iw-search/we/InfoWeb?p_action=doc&p_docid=0EB599B1, July 22, 2008.

19   "very alone," resented by . . . because she had a match.": Fitzhenry, "Reece Shares Her Life."

19   her perturbation over the fact . . . and a volleyball player second.: Fitzhenry, "Reece Shares Her Life."

20   "notorious for his catnaps . . . and any place.": Bowden with Ellis, p. 134.

20   Defensive coordinator Mickey Andrews . . . and ready to go.": Bowden with Ellis, p. 135.

20   Immediately before the 1989 game . . . relaxed their coach was.: Bowden with Ellis, p. 136.

20   I can really see the value . . . wherever I am, I'm asleep.: Bettinger, p. 88.

21   Thomas was one of four . . . desegregation were crumbling.: Schlabach, p. 132.

21   "an awesome thing.": Schlabach, p. 134.

21   "I was taking on the burden . . . in the newspapers,": Schlabach, p. 134.

21   "everybody started cheering . . . in the same formation": Schlabach, p. 136.

21   "I couldn't have asked for a better ending to the game,": Schlabach, p. 136.

22   A Chicago native, Kinderman . . . before the 1961 season.: Schlabach, p. 51.

22   He played in six games: Schlabach, p. 53.

22   led the team with 393 yards rushing: Schlabach, p. 55.

22   After a night at some . . . 1953 Mercury hit the road.: Schlabach, p. 53.

22   I've seen people change . . . human beings through faith.: Bettinger, p. 46.

23   "the biggest win in school history": "FSU Soccer Stuns UNC," *Tallahassee Democrat*, Nov. 25, 2005, p. C, http://infoweb.newsbank.com/iw-search/we/

Info?Web?p_action=doc&p_docid=10E2387E0, July 22, 2008.

23   fending off 31 Carolina . . . to pull Mims for Pyykko.: Randy Beard, "Few Details Escape FSU Soccer Coach Krikorian," *Tallahassee Democrat*, Nov. 30, 2005, p. c1, http://infoweb.newsbank.com/iw-search/we/InfoWeb?p_ action=doc&p_docid=10E38A00, July 22, 2008.

23   Pyykko stopped the second . . . on the penalty kicks.: Beard, "Few Details Escape."

23   His staff and he . . . her left leg in 2002.: Beard, "Few Details Escape."

24   In 1980, Hernandez and his mother . . . We saw the sea swallow them.": Long, p. 108.

24   No one knows when he . . . blink of an eye.: Bettinger, p. 21.

25   The next-best record during . . . at least four times.: Long, pp. 13-14.

25   "When I die, . . . he played Miami.": Long, p. 126.

26   Simon saw the team losing . . . help his team win a championship.: Jack Corcoran, "Determined to Lead," *Tallahassee Democrat*, Nov. 20, 1999, p. F10, http://infoweb.newsbank.com/iw-search/we/InfoWeb?p_ action=doc&p_docid=0EB59A71, July 23, 2008.

26   I have an obligation to set . . . an example in . . . language.: Bettinger, p. 25.

27   It wasn't just the lights . . . promises and no guarantees.": John Nogowski, "Sura Ignores Call of NBA's Lights to Help Team," *Tallahassee Democrat*, April 14, 1994, p. 1C, http://infoweb.newsbank.com/iw-search/we/ InfoWeb?p_action=doc&p_docid=0EB598A5, July 22, 2008.

27   Sura had a dream. . . . 38-year-old record.: Nogowski, "Sura Ignores Call."

28   Somebody was trying to . . . that's just not true.": John Nogwoski, "Have Mercy?" *Tallahassee Democrat*, Oct. 4, 1997, p. 1A, http://infoweb.newsbank. com/iw-search/we/InfoWeb?p_action=doc&p_docid=0EB599C1, July 23, 2008.

28   "Take it easy on . . . their hopes and dreams,": Nogowski, "Have Mercy?"

28   "crippling NCAA scholarship-reduction . . . the NCAA rulebook.": Nogowski, "Have Mercy?"

28   "Those of us who . . . what the final score is,": Nogowski, "Have Mercy?"

29   When Graf first suited up . . . showpiece of a softball complex.: Mark Fitzhenry, "FSU Women's Softball Pitches Graf Toward Her 900th Win," *Tallahassee Democrat*, April 4, 1997, p. 1A, http://infoweb.newsbank.com/iw-search/we/InfoWeb?p_action=doc&p_docid=0EB59997, July 22, 2008.

29   Even after a day of . . . "to do the next day.": Fitzhenry, "FSU Women's Softball Pitches Graf."

30   The media recognize FSU's . . . fast-break, no-huddle offense,: Bobby Bowden with Steve Ellis, p. 42.

30   the success of the offense run . . . "take it up a notch.": Bowden with Ellis, p. 41.

30   "We're playing conventional offense . . . and see what happens.": Bowden with Ellis, p. 43.

30   "Boy, that Charlie was something out of that shotgun.": Bowden with Ellis, p. 44.

30   Scott and Richt visited . . . scheme to protect Ward.: Bowden with Ellis, p. 42.

30   "Here my old man is . . . won him a national championship.": Bowden with Ellis, p. 44.

30   Dad is a great example . . . to make a change.: Bowden with Ellis, p. 45.

31   *Sports Illustrated* declared in . . . never a halftime show.": "Our History," *Marching Chiefs: The Largest College Marching Band*, http://www.marchingchiefs.fsu.edu/index.php, July 14, 2008.

31   The forerunner of today's band . . . at Stetson University in 1949.: "Our History."

31   "The Hymn to the Garnet . . . produce its own CD.: "Our History."

31   I would like to think . . . to have been a bandleader.: Bettinger, p. 36.

32   Bowden's immediate concern was . . . "So I'm thinking, 'No sweat.'", Bowden with Ellis, p. 10.

32   But then an official told . . . five yards out of it.": Bowden with Ellis, p. 11.

32   We won twice.: Bowden with Ellis, p. 13.

33   He was such a campus . . . tune of "Hello, Dolly.": "Fred 'Freddie B.' Biletnikoff," *National Football Foundation's College Football Hall of Fame*, http://www.collegefootball.org/famersearch.php?id=60004, July 26, 2008.

33   "Fred Biletnikoff cut neither . . . in many different configurations.": Long, p. 78.

33   He wore loose sleeves and baggy socks,: Long, p. 78.

33   hand cut his uniform to his liking,: "1965-78 Fred Biletnikoff," *Helmet Hut: Oakland Raiders*, http://www.helmethut.com/biletnikoff.html, July 26, 2008.

33   blackened his eyes,: Long, p. 78.

33   saturated his hands and . . . a number of broken noses.: *Helmet Hut.*

33   "The thinning, dirty-blond . . . to his raggedy appearance.": Long, p. 78.

34   Her mother became ill, . . . became the one.: Jack Corcoran, "Have Faith," *Tallahassee Democrat*, Nov. 13, 2998, p. 6B, http://infoweb.newsbank.com/iw-search/we/InfoWeb?p_action=doc&p_docid=0EB59A1A, July 23, 2008.

34   "This is where God . . . out of the blue.": Corcoran, "Have Faith."

35   "arguably the most consequential recruit in FSU's neophyte football history.": Long, p. 73.

35   Coach Tom Nugent persuaded . . . at schools such as Clemson.": Schlabach, p. 10.

35   Corso had led the team . . . with 14 career interceptions.: Schlabach, p. 13.

35   Before his sophomore season, . . . misdiagnosed as a sprain.: Schlabach, p. 12.

36   "A phone call saves . . . wild goose chase—.": Bowden with Ellis, p. 124.

36   Wally Burnham once took . . . signed with Notre Dame.: Bowden with Ellis, p. 125.

37   Adams' dorm was an Air Force . . . "spartan but quite satisfactory.": Schlabach, pp. 2-3.

37   The team traveled to road games in an old school bus.: Schlabach, p. 7.

37   Since he was from Tallahassee . . . living at home.: Schlabach, p. 6.

37   When FSU went to Selma . . . tough getting a call.": Schlabach, p. 7.

37   "It was a big deal . . . for other people.": Schlabach, pp. 4-5.

38   "forever cemented his place . . . make sure it's a three.": David Lee Simmons, "A Shot Heard All Over," *Tallahassee Democrat*, Feb. 23, 1994, p. 1C, http://infoweb.newsbank.com/iw-search/we/InfoWeb?p_action=doc&p_docid=0EB59896, July 22, 2008.

38   I had a good alibi . . . and win the game.: Bettinger, p. 116.

39   the Noles were tied at . . . have plenty of time.": Bowden with Ellis, p. 56.

39	after watching Southern Miss . . . to the FSU 25: Bowden with Ellis, p. 56.
40	the Jayhawks reached the . . . didn't' break the plane.: Steve Ellis, *Seminole Glory* (Tallahassee: *Tallahassee Democrat*, 2003), p. 16.
40	"It was probably the best . . . Simply embarrassing,": Ellis, *Seminole Glory*, p. 18.
40	It's amazing. . . . a Christian man.: Bettinger, p. 121.
41	That's when it started . . . included his mom and dad": John Nogowski, "Mientkiewicz, Parents Pull off Happy Ending," *Tallahassee Democrat*, May 29, 1995, p. 1B, http://infoweb.newsbank.com/iw-search/we/InfoWeb?p_action=doc&p_docid=0EB598FA, July 22, 2008.
42	FSU led 14-13 . . . remained one of his favorites.: Bowden with Ellis, pp. 48-49.
43	On the night of Nov. 25, . . . watching out for that guy.": Jill Palermo, "With Some Field Dressing, FSU Football Players Help Save Student," *Tallahassee Democrat*, Nov. 26, 1996, p. 1A, http://infoweb.newsbank.com/iw-search/we/InfoWeb?p_action=doc&p_docid=0EB59976, July 23, 2008.
44	taking a 14-0 lead . . . to wideout Greg Carr.: Tim Layden, "Seminole Moment," *Sports Illustrated*, Sept. 26, 2005, http://vault.sportsillustrated.cnn.com/vault/article/magazine/MAG1104574/index.htm, July 14, 2008.
44	They rallied to lead . . . a five-yard TD pass to Carr.: Layden, "Seminole Moment."
45	the women's teams at FSU had no budgets . . . FSU's first full-time women's athletic director.: Gerald Ensley, "A Sporting Chance," *Tallahassee Democrat*, March 26, 1995, p. 1D, http://infoweb.newsbank.com/iw-search/we/InfoWeb?p_action=doc&p_docid=0EB598ED, July 22, 2008.
46	Against Georgia, the Seminoles . . . He never ran the ball.: Schlabach, p. 75.
46	"I probably ran the ball . . . But it worked.": Schlabach, p. 76.
46	God doesn't want . . . wants your availability.: Bettinger, p. 108.
47	Butler was born so . . . his legs would heal.": Michael Silver, "Stepping Out, " *Sports Illustrated*, May 19, 1997, http://vault.sportsillustrated.cnn.com/vault/article/magazine/MAG1010101/1/index.htm, July 14, 2008.
47	who wore the same kind of braces Butler did.: "LeRoy Butler," *Answers.com*, http://www.answers.com/topic/leroy-butler, July 28, 2008.
47	When LeRoy was eight, . . . his first kickball game.: Silver.
48	Bobby Bowden learned a valuable . . . circumstances in November 1976.: Bowden with Ellis, p. 17.
48	"probably my all-time favorite game in 28 years.": Bowden with Ellis, p. 14.
48	The situation got worse . . . but have fun.": Bowden with Ellis, p. 14.
48	"goes down in history . . . he had the touchdown.: Bowden with Ellis, p. 16.
48	Bowden reinforced the lesson . . . roll down a snow bank.: Bowden with Ellis, p. 17.
49	It got so bad he . . . midway through the season.: Steve Ellis, "Healed by Faith in God," *Tallahassee Democrat*, Feb. 14, 2001, p. C1, http://infoweb.newsbank.com/iw-search/we/InfoWeb?p_action=doc&p_docid=0EB5986C, July 23, 2008.
49	But FSU football players . . . hour of pain-free basketball.: Ellis, "Healed by Faith in God."
49	"People can reason with me . . . I believe.": Ellis, 'Healed by Faith in God."

49   If faith healing is what it took, . . . it's cool.: Ellis, "Healed by Faith in God."

50   "Bill Peterson achieved . . . a stand-up comedian.": Hubert Mizell, "Peterson Legacy: Coaches," *St. Petersburg Times*, Aug. 6, 1993, p. 1C, http://pqasb. pqarchiver.com/sptimes/access/51730682. html, July 21, 2008.

50   Peterson earned the reputation . . . Kim Hammond, and Ron Sellers.: Long, p. 74.

50   "David needed some help . . . days and days and days.": Long, p. 76.

51   Jon Nance could have been . . . Chuck Amato, said so.: Jim Lamar, "Against the Odds," *Tallahassee Democrat*, Dec. 31, 1993, p. 1C, http://infoweb.newsbank.com/iw-search/we/InfoWeb?p_action=doc&p_docid=0EB59886, July 22, 2008.

51   Nance played only one . . . missing much of his senior season.: Lamar.

51   "I feel like I'm blessed," . . . had that positive attitude.": Lamar.

52   In the summer of 1997 before . . . basketball for FSU anymore.: Mark Fitzhenry, "She's Happy with Tough Choice," *Tallahassee Democrat*, Dec. 4, 1997, p. 1C, http://infoweb.com/iw-search/we/InfoWeb?p_action=doc&p_docid=0EB599D0, July 22, 2008.

52   Slowly, Coleman changed her mind . . . now, having a ball.": Fitzhenry, "She's Happy."

53   the only Heisman-Trophy winner . . . and seven ACC records: "Charlie Ward," *Wikipedia, the free encyclopedia*, http://en.wikipedia.org/wiki/Charlie_Ward.

53   When he was a senior, . . . I've been all my life.": Rick Reilly, "A Gentleman and a Scholar," *Sports Illustrated*, Dec. 27, 1993. http://vault.sportsillustrated.ccn.com/vault/article/magazine/MAG1138130/index.htm, July 14, 2008.

54   ends Jim Costello and Chris . . . fullback Jack Watson.: Ben, p. 52.

54   Life is an adventure . . . to happen next.: Bettinger, p. 74.

55   On May 25, 1995, Calkins was asleep . . . drew closer to God.: Mark Fitzhenry, "Accident Puts Calkins' Life in Focus," *Tallahassee Democrat*, Feb. 12, 1997, p. 1C, http://infoweb.newsbank.com/iw-search/we/InfoWeb?p_action=doc&p_docid=0EB5998A, July 22, 2008.

55   "made me enjoy softball . . . It's a game." Fitzhenry, "Accident Puts Calkins' Life."

55   "FSU's most complete player ever.": Fitzhenry: "Accident Puts Calkins' Life."

56   When Bowden arrived in Tallahassee . . . just "beat somebody.": Ben, p. 19.

56   "After we beat somebody . . . have a winning season,": Ben, p. 20.

56   Have a winning season *and* beat Florida.: Ben, p. 21.

56   could we just get a bowl bid?: Ben, p. 22.

56   a top-ten ranking: Ben, p. 27.

56   *and* a major bowl bid: Ben, p. 23.

56   could we just *win* a major bowl?: Ben, p. 24.

56   win the national championship!: Ben, pp. 28-29.

56   I want to win . . . in the United States.: Bettinger, p. 66.

57   The FSU men's basketball media . . . player in school history.: *FSU Seminole Basketball Media Guide: 2006-2007*, p. 197, www.seminoles.com.

57   he was introduced as . . . represented Miami.: Randy Beard, "Cowens Has ACC Legacy for One Day," *Tallahassee Democrat*, March 13, 2005, p. C1, http://infoweb.newsbank.com/iw-search/we/InfoWeb?p_action=doc&p_

docid=108D2F8E, July 23, 2008.

58   He's got a hundred pounds of meanness that don't show.": Steve Ellis, "Original 'Nole Jack Tully Dies," *Tallahassee Democrat*, March 9, 2008, p. C1, http://infoweb.newsbank.com/iw-search/we/InfoWeb?p_action=doc&p_docid=11F5F1DB, July 23, 2008.

58   "He was a fighter and a leader . . . Green Bay Packer Ray Nitschke,": Ellis, "Original 'Nole Jack Tully Dies."

59   "one of the lowest periods of my life.": Long, p. 18.

59   "became a career pothole . . . sinkhole by critics": Long, p. 17.

59   Bowden couldn't recall . . . contracts to one year.: Long, p. 18.

59   When Bowden came to Tampa . . . coming to Tallahassee.: Long, p. 18.

60   With only thirteen minutes . . . made it a 31-30 game.: Long, p. 130.

60   "I can't afford to blow this . . . Let's ensure a tie.": Bowden with Steve Ellis, p. 31.

60   "We did something unprecedented. . . . sweet as a victory.": Bowden with Ellis, p. 31.

60   Linebacker Todd Rebol realized . . . that almost happened.": Long, p. 131.

60   "It's a tie, but . . . it felt like a win.": Bowden with Ellis, p. 31.

61   Mat "was kind of the . . . emerged as a top player.": Corey Clark, "Cloer Makes His Own Way at FSU," *Tallahassee Democrat*, May 16, 2008, p. C1, http://infoweb.newsbank.com/iw-search/we/InfoWeb?p_action=doc&p_docid=120BC24E, July 23, 2008.

61   He heard "oh, that's . . . heart and soul of this team.": Clark.

62   "Everything I heard all week was negative, negative, negative,": Tim Layden, "Razing Canes," *Sports Illustrated*, Oct. 21, 1996, http://vault.sportsillustrated.ccn.com/vault/article/magazine/MAG1008912/index.htm, July 14, 2008.

62   "I didn't want to let . . . Throw and catch.": Layden, "Razing Canes."

62   I think God made it . . . accept Him and believe.: Bettinger, p. 47.

63   Halina Janikowski cried bitterly . . . really bad every time.": Tim Layden, "Big Foot," *Sports Illustrated*, Dec. 20, 1999, http://vault.sportsillustrated.cnn.com/vault/article/magazine/MAG1017978/index.htm, July 14, 2008.

63   he brought his mother to America.: "Sebastian Janikowski, *JockBio.com*, http://www.jockbio.com/Bios/Janikowski/Janikowski_numbers.html, July 27, 2008.

63   I was a momma's boy.: Bettinger, p. 18.

64   "After I ran that 7.15, . . . "was extremely scared.": Jack Corcoran, "FSU's Carter Overcomes Pressure to Win NCAA," *Tallahassee Democrat*, March 15, 2000, p. C5, http://infoweb.newsbank.com/iw-search/we/InfoWeb?p_action=docid=0EB59807, July 22, 2008.

64   First she prayed. . . . "Please, God," she said.: Corcoran, "FSU's Carter."

64   About halfway through the race, . . . Just get out and run.": Corcoran, "FSU's Carter."

64   The Good Lord might not . . . after the pilot.: Bettinger, p. 55.

65   Weinke led the Noles . . . remove the herniated disk.: Long, p. 45.

65   Within days, though, he was . . . if he moved quickly.: Long, pp. 45-46.

66   An inspired alumnus wrote a poem titled "Huff the Magic Dragon.": Barry McDermott, "The Magic Dragon Is Joust About the Best," *Sports Illustrated*, Sept. 25, 1972, http://vault.sports

illustrated.ccn.com/vault/article/magazine/MAG1086565/index.htm, July 14, 2008.

66 Smith caught a 66-yard . . . going to like this guy.": Schlabach, p. 123.

66 Houston was waxing the Noles . . . never knew what hit him,": Schlabach, p. 124.

66 "I probably dropped two or three . . . I was the goat.": Schlabach, p. 126.

66 I've been a hero . . . hero a lot better.: Bettinger, p. 72.

67 Loucks had no assistant coaches . . . starred in football and tennis.: Gerald Ensley, "Remembering FSU's First Win 48 Years Later," *Tallahassee Democrat*, Dec. 11, 1995, p. 1B, http://infoweb.newsbank.com/iw-search/we/InfoWeb?p_action=doc&p_docid=0EB59922, July 23, 2008.

68 60 Divide was a play . . . 'What did he say?' '60 Divide.'": Bowden with Ellis, p. x.

69 Bowden had to break . . . heard about the shooting.: Bowden with Ellis, p. 166.

69 "the worst thing to happen . . . a conclusive cause of death.: Bowden with Ellis, p. 167.

69 In 1990 shortly before . . . my heart sunk,": Bowden with Ellis, pp. 170-71.

70 "People used to laugh . . . He lives that every day.": W. Frank Allen, "Faith on the Field," *Tallahassee Democrat*, Feb. 15, 1997, p. 1C, http://infoweb.newsbank.com/iw-search/we/InfoWeb?p_action=doc&p_docid=0EB5998B, July 22, 2008.

70 I used to say you . . . further from the truth.: Allen.

71 The Noles rolled up more . . . Doak Campbell Stadium after games.: Steve Ellis, "The Streak," *Tallahassee Democrat*, Oct. 8, 2001, p. C8, http://infoweb.newsbacnk.com/iw-search/we/InfoWeb?p_action=do&p_docid=0EF699801, July 23, 2008.

72 As the coaches assembled their . . . yielded to McDuffie's vision and persistence.: Gerald Ensley, "McDuffie's Vision," *Tallahassee Democrat*, Dec. 12, 1993, p. 3B, http://infoweb.newsbank.com/iw-search/we/InfoWeb?p_action=doc&p_docid=0EB59881, July 22, 2008.

73 and didn't get to travel . . . about being on scholarship,": Schlabach, p. 301.

73 I have no prejudices . . . I will eat anything.: Bettinger, p. 114.

74 Kimmy Carter knew she . . . Why don't you try catching?": Jack Corcoran, "The Kid's Kid: FSU Freshman Kimmy Carter, Daughter of Former Professional Baseball Player Gary Carter, Has Found a Home," *Tallahassee Democrat*, May 14, 1999, p. 1B, http://infoweb.newsbank.com/iw-search/we/InfoWeb?p_action=doc&p_docid=0EB59A43, July 22, 2008.

74 So she found some . . . gear just looked funny.": Corcoran, "The Kid's Kid."

74 "Anytime I needed help, all I had to do was ask him,": Corcoran, "The Kid's Kid."

74 "From a father standpoint, . . . on fire for the Lord.": Corcoran, "The Kid's Kid."

75 When he was 84 . . . "Those were the days,": Brad Milner, "From War to Lore," *newsherald.com*, Dec. 19, 2007, http://www.newsherald.com/sports/_2043_article.html/.html, Aug. 21, 2008.

76 coach Mike Martin knew . . . didn't play like a freshman.": Derek Redd, "Florida State Catcher Buster Posey Takes Center Stage," *Palm Beach Post*, May 29, 2008, http://www.palmbeachpost.com/sports/content/sports/

epaper/2008/05/29/0530fsu.html, Aug. 21, 2008.

76   The Noles needed a catcher . . . finalist for the Johnny Bench Award,: Redd.

76   a situation Martin admitted he had never had before.: Corey Clark, "Posey as Catcher-Closer Unique Situation for FSU Coach Martin," *Tallahassee Democrat*, March 1, 2008, p. C2, http://infoweb.newsbank.com/iw-search/we/InfoWeb?p_action=doc&p_docid=11F3A608, July 23, 2008.

76   the fourth player . . . positions in a game.: Steve Ellis, "All the Field Is Posey's Stage," *Tallahassee Democrat*, May 13, 2008, p. C1, http://infoweb.newsbank.com/iw-search/we/InfoWeb?p_action=doc&p_docid=120AB43D, July 23, 2008.

77   as the Seminoles rolled up . . . for running up the score.: Ashley McGeachy, "End Zone Madness," *Sports Illustrated*, Sept. 25, 1995, http://vault.sportsillustrated.cnn.com/vault/article/magafzine/MAG 1007152/index.htm, July 16, 2008.

77   Charlie Ward broke Gary Huff's total career yardage.: Ellis, *Seminole Glory*, p. 114.

77   the Gamecock fans behind the FSU bench . . . such a lame performance.": Long, p. 91.

77   Do you really mind . . . to your sons? Schlabach, p. ix.

78   "I wouldn't do that any differently.": Bowden with Ellis, p. 36.

78   "Right now I would kick . . . told them they should have kicked.: Bowden with Ellis, p. 36.

78   "I felt like I had let them down,": Bowden with Ellis, p. 37.

78   "I felt that wasn't necessary,": Bowden with Ellis, p. 36.

78   Tailback Sammie Smith . . . feel a little better.: Bowden with Ellis, p. 37.

78   The only regret I have . . . . play for Bobby Bowden.: Bettinger, p. 124.

79   "watching the team get off the van . . . by four power players,: Jim Sumner, "Looking Back: 1981 Seminoles Power Through to a National Championship," *theACC.com*, May 9, 2007, http://www.theacc.com/sports/w-golf/spec-rel/050907aac.html, July 28, 2008.

79   after two rounds, the Noles . . . rings from the athletic department.: Sumner.

80   "People who might think . . . what's inside of me.": Long, p. 101.

80   At a party in high school . . . too easy to go along.: Long, pp. 100-01.

80   his momma's "last hope": Long, p. 100.

80   "despicable, vile, unprincipled scoundrels.": John MacArthur, *Twelve Ordinary Men* (Nashville: W Publishing Group, 2002), p. 152.

80   Football is a way . . . what he was raised in.: Long, p. 101.

81   "Rodney Dangerfield of FSU coaches,": "Darrell Mudra, the Rodney Dangerfield of FSU Coaches," *garnetandgreat.com*, Feb. 15, 2008, http://classic-noles.typepad.com/garnetandgreat, Aug. 18, 2008.

81   There was no weight room . . . could study and eat together.: "Darrell Mudra."

81   He once told Mudra . . . turned the program around,: "Darrell Mudra."

81   We took over a program that was really in disarray.: "Darrell Mudra."

82   when North Carolina scored 21 . . . as talented as the Tar Heels.: Randy Beard, "Pickett Performs Miracle," *Tallahassee Democrat*, Jan. 23, 2004, p. C1, http://infoweb.newsbank.com/

83 iw-search/we/InfoWeb?p_action=doc&p_docid=100FBFAB, July 23, 2008.

83 Martin's 1994 baseball team . . . for Florida State University.": John Nogowski, "Martin Stands up for His True FSU Beliefs," *Tallahassee Democrat*, May 18, 1994, p. 1B, http://infoweb.newsbank.com/iw-search/we/InfoWeb?p_action=doc&p_docid=0EB598AD, July 22, 2008.

83 I won't tolerate a womanizer. . . . cost you your job.: Bettinger, p. 26.

84 On Oct. 18, 1947, Don Grant . . . while 7,165 fans watched": "A Brief History."

84 before 9,676 fans. . . . in only five months: "A Brief History."

84 at a cost of . . . capacity was 15,000.: "Bobby Bowden Field at Doak Campbell Stadium," *Seminole Football: 2007 Florida State Media Guide*, www.seminoles.com, p. 195.

84 Tallahasseean Rainey Cawthon . . . $1 an hour for their work.: "A Brief History."

84 Nine expansions: "Bobby Bowden Field," p. 195.

84 The south end zone . . . golf green standards.: "Bobby Bowden Field," p. 194.

85 "like a man chasing a mirage in the desert.": John Nogowski, "Bowden Finally Has His Trophy," *Tallahassee Democrat*, Jan. 3, 1994, p. 1A, http://infoweb.newsbank.com/iw-search/we/InfoWeb?p_action=doc&p_docid=0EB59889, July 23, 2008.

85 "We were number three . . . up ahead of us?" Long, p. 107.

85 Bowden said he wasn't losing . . . from the jaws of victory.": Nogowski, "Bowden Finally Has His Trophy."

85 After getting so close . . . ever get to come here.": Bettinger, p. 91.

86 The helmet was a piece . . . provided them himself.: Clyde Bolton, *The Crimson Tide* (The Strode Publishers: Huntsville, AL, 1972), p. 46.

86 Hiding the ball under a jersey.: Clyde Bolton, *War Eagle* (The Strode Publishers: Huntsville, AL, 1973), p. 69.

86 Using his helmet for a tee.: Bolton, *War Eagle*, p. 78.

86 Spectators rushing . . . in the players' way.: Bolton, *War Eagle*, p. 49.

86 Players dragging ball carriers forward.: Bolton, *War Eagle*, p. 76.

86 Linemen holding hands . . . before a play began.: Bolton, *The Crimson Tide*, p. 47.

86 Darkness forcing games to be called.: Bolton, *War Eagle*, p. 48.

86 Teams deciding upon . . . once they showed up.: Bolton, *War Eagle*, p. 80.

86 when handles were sewn . . . easier to toss.: Bolton, *War Eagle*, p. 76.

87 "remember me for what . . . messed up off the field.": Long, p. 6.

87 "What do y'all . . . want me to finish 'em?" Long, p. 1.

87 Guard Jason Whitaker later verified . . . the linemen's response:: Long, p. 9.

87 "Finish 'em, Pete.": Long, p. 1.

87 With a Tech defender sprinting . . . secure the ball to his body.": Long, p. 9.

88 Everything is routine . . . used to the pain.": Mark Fitzhenry, "Playing Through the Pain," *Tallahassee Democrat*, Dec. 16, 1997, p. 1B, http://infoweb.newsbank.com/iw-search/we/InfoWeb?p_action=doc&p_docid=0EB599D3, July 23, 2008.

88 "a second look virtually . . . can't play basketball again.": Fitzhenry, "Playing Through the Pain."

89 "When he hits people, . . . Oh, it's lovely.'": Sally Jenkins, "Made in the

Shade," *Sports Illustrated*, April 26, 1993, http://vault.sportsillustrated.cnn.com/vault/article/magazine/MAG1138115/index.htm, July 14, 2008.

89	"a little-boy-lost quality." . . . have a talkative relationship.": Jenkins.
90	"I don't like 'yes' men," . . . you get yourself beat.": Bowden with Ellis, p. 143.
90	the "most controversial" guy he ever worked with.: Bowden with Ellis, p. 143.
90	"a tough nut, but I loved him.": Bowden with Ellis, p. 140.
90	"the most demonstrative of . . . Bowden's play calling.": Bowden with Ellis, p. 142.
90	McDuffie left the press box . . . Noles were still playing.: Bowden with Ellis, p. 140.
90	"The only thing I could . . . kind of the standard answer.": Bowden with Ellis, pp. 141-42.
90	During the 1985 Auburn game, . . . get it in fourth and one.": Bowden with Ellis, p. 143.

BIBLIOGRAPHY

"1965-78 Fred Biletnikoff." *Helmet Hut: Oakland Raiders.* http://www.helmethut.com/biletnikoff.html.

"1981 & 1982 National Champions." *Florida State University: 2008 Seminole Softball.* 69. www.seminoles.com.

Allen, W. Frank. "Faith on the Field: Coach Mike Martin Knows There's More to Life than Baseball." *Tallahassee Democrat.* 15 Feb. 1997. 1C. http://infoweb.newsbank.com/iw-search/we/InfoWeb?p_action=doc&p_docid=0EB5998B.

Beard, Randy. "Cowens Has ACC Legacy for One Day." *Tallahassee Democrat.* 13 March 2005. C1. http://infoweb.newsbank.com/iw-search/we/InfoWeb?p_action=doc&p_docid=108D2F8F.

---. "Few Details Escape FSU Soccer Coach Krikorian." *Tallahassee Democrat.* 30 Nov. 2005. C1. http://infoweb.newsbank.com/iw-search/we/InfoWeb?p_action=doc&p_docid=10E38A00.

---. "Pickett Performs Miracle." *Tallahassee Democrat.* 23 Jan. 2004. C1. http://infoweb.newsbank.com/iw-search/we/InfoWeb?p_action=doc&p_docid=100FBFAB.

Bechtel, Mark. "Heavy Metal Rap." *Sports Illustrated.* 13 March 2000. http://vault.sportsillustrated.cnn.com/vault/article/magazine/MAG1018533/index.htm.

Ben, Philip L. *Seminole Gold: Fifty Years of Sports at Florida State.* Marietta, GA: Longstreet Press, Inc., 1996.

Bettinger, Jim & Julie S. *The Book of Bowden.* Nashville: TowleHouse Publishing, 2001.

"Bobby Bowden Field at Doak Campbell Stadium." *Seminole Football: 2007 Florida State Media Guide.* www.seminoles.com. 194-95.

Bolton, Clyde. *The Crimson Tide: A Story of Alabama Football.* Huntsville, AL: The Strode Publishers, 1972.

---. *War Eagle: A Story of Auburn Football.* Huntsville, AL: The Strode Publishers, 1973.

Bowden, Bobby with Steve Ellis. *Bobby Bowden's Tales from the Seminoles Sidelines.* Champaign, IL: Sports Publishing L.L.C, 2004.

"A Brief History of Florida State Football." *Seminole Football: 2007 Florida State Media Guide.* www.seminoles.com. 204.

"Charlie Ward." *Wikipedia, the free encyclopedia.* http://en.wikipedia.org/wiki/Charlie_Ward.

Clark, Corey. "Cloer Makes His Own Way at FSU." *Tallahassee Democrat.* 16 May 2008. C1. http://infoweb.newsbank.com/iw-search/we/InfoWeb?p_action=doc&p_docid=120BC24F.

---. "Loyalty Lets FSU Track Star Dix Cash In." *Tallahassee Democrat.* 10 July 2008. http://nolesports.tallahassee.com/apps/pbcs.dll/article?AID=/20080710/FSU09/807100336.

---. "Posey as Catcher-Closer Unique Situation for FSU Coach Martin." *Tallahassee Democrat.* 1 March 2008. C2. http://infoweb.newsbank.com/iw-search/we/InfoWeb?p_action=doc&p_docid=11F3A608.

Corcoran, Jack. "Determined to Lead." *Tallahassee Democrat.* 20 Nov. 1999. F10. http://infoweb.newsbank.com/iw-search/we/InfoWeb?p_action=doc&p_docid=0EB59A71.

---. "FSU's Carter Overcomes Pressure to Win NCAA." *Tallahassee Democrat.* 15 March 2000. C5. http://infoweb.newsbank.com/iw-search/we/InfoWeb?p_action=doc&p_docid=0EB59807.

---. "Have Faith: Gracey Adds to Improved 'Noles." *Tallahassee Democrat.* 13 Nov. 1998. 6B. http://infoweb.newsbank.com/iw-search/we/InfoWeb?p_action=doc&p_docid+0EB59A1A.

---. "The Kid's Kid: FSU Freshman Kimmy Carter, Daughter of Former Professional Baseball Player Gary Carter, Has Found a Home." *Tallahassee Democrat.* 14 May 1999. 1B. http://infoweb.newsbank.com/iw-search/we/InfoWeb?p_action=doc&p_docid=0EB59A43.

Culpepper, R. Alan. "The Gospel of Luke: Introduction, Commentary, and Reflections." *The New Interpreter's Bible.* Nashville: Abingdon Press, 1995. Vol. IX. 1-490. http://infoweb.newsbank.com/iw-search/we/InfoWeb?p_action=doc&p_docid=0EB59A1A.

"Darrell Mudra, the Rodney Dangerfield of FSU Coaches." *garnetandgreat.com.* 15 Feb. 2008. http://classicnoles.typepad.com/garnetandgreat.

Ellis, Steve. "All the Field Is Posey's Stage." *Tallahassee Democrat.* 13 May 2008. C1. http://infoweb.newsbank.com/iw-search/we/InfoWeb?p_action=doc&p_docid=120AB43D.

---. "Healed by Faith in God." *Tallahassee Democrat.* 14 Feb. 2001. C1. http://infoweb.newsbank.com/iw-search/we/InfoWeb?p_action=doc&p_docid=0EB5986C.

---. "Original 'Nole Jack Tully Dies." *Tallahassee Democrat.* 9 March 2008. C1. http://infoweb.newsbank.com/iw-search/we/InfoWeb?p_action=doc&p_docid=11F5F1DB.

---. *Seminole Glory: A Look Back at Florida State's 1993 Championship Season.* Tallahassee: Tallahassee Democrat, 2003.

---. "The Streak." *Tallahassee Democrat.* 8 Oct. 2001. C8. http://infoweb.newsbacnk.com/iw-search/we/InfoWeb?p_action=doc&p_docid=0EF699801.

Ensley, Gerald. "McDuffie's Vision: It's Unlikely Charlie Ward Would Have Come to FSU Without the Persistence of a Former FSU Assistant Coach." *Tallahassee Democrat.* 12 Dec. 1993. 3B. http://infoweb.newsbank.com/iw-search/we/InfoWeb?p_action=doc&p_docid=0EB59881.

---. "Remembering FSU's First Win 48 Years Later." *Tallahassee Democrat.* 11 Dec. 1995. 1B. http://infoweb.newsbank.com/iw-search/we/InfoWeb?p_action=doc&p_docid=0EB59922.

---. "Show of 'Sportsmanship' Endures." *Tallahassee Democrat*. 4 Dec. 2000. B1. http://infoweb.newsbank.com/iw-search/we/InfoWeb?p_action=doc&p_docid=0EB5985B.

---. "A Sporting Chance: It Was an Era of Hard Work That Yielded High Returns." *Tallahassee Democrat*. 26 March 1995. 1D. http://infoweb.newsbank.com/iw-search/we/InfoWeb?p_action=doc&p_docid=0EB598ED.

Fitzhenry, Mark. "Accident Puts Calkins' Life in Focus." *Tallahassee Democrat*. 12 Feb. 1997. 1C. http://infoweb.newsbank.com/iw-search/we/InfoWeb?p_action=doc&p_docid=0EB5998A.

---. "FSU Women's Softball Pitches Graf Toward Her 900th Win." *Tallahassee Democrat*. 4 April 1997. 1A. http://infoweb.newsbank.com/iw-search/we/InfoWeb?p_action=doc&p_docid=0EB59997.

---. "Playing Through the Pain: Severe Pain Caused by 'Black Line Syndrome' Isn't Keeping Arleshia Davidson Away from the Game She Loves." *Tallahassee Democrat*. 16 Dec. 1997. 1B. http://infoweb.newsbank.com/iw-search/we/InfoWeb?p_action=doc&p_docid=0EB599D3.

---. "Reece Shares Her Life as a 'Big Girl': The Sports Superstar Examines Her Competitive Edge in a New Book." *Tallahassee Democrat*. 27 July 1997. 1E. http://infoweb.newsbank.com/iw-search/we/InfoWeb?p_action=doc&p_docid=0EB599B1.

---. "She's Happy with Tough Choice: After Considering Leaving, Latavia Coleman Decided to Stay at FSU." *Tallahassee Democrat*. 4 Dec. 1997. 1C. http://infoweb.newsbank.com/iw-search/we/InfoWeb?p_action=doc&p_docid=0EB599D0.

"Fred 'Freddie B.' Biletnikoff." *National Football Foundation's College Football Hall of Fame*. http://www.collegefootball.org/famersearch.php?id=60004.

FSU *Seminole Basketball Media Guide: 2006-2007*. www.seminoles.com.

"FSU Soccer Stuns UNC." *Tallahassee Democrat*. 25 Nov. 2005. C. http://infoweb.newsbank.com/iw-search/we/InfoWeb?p_action=doc&p_docid=10E2387E0.

"Gabrielle Reece." *Wikipedia, the free encyclopedia*. http://en.wikipedia.org/wiki/Gabrielle_Reece.

Jenkins, Sally. "Made in the Shade." *Sports Illustrated*. 26 April 1993. http://vault.sportsillustrated.cnn.com/vault/article/magazine/MAG1138115/index.htm.

Lamar, Jim. "Against the Odds: Despite Illness and Injury, Jon Nance Has Maintained a Positive Attitude." *Tallahassee Democrat*. 31 Dec. 1993. 1C. http://infoweb.newsbank.com/iw-search/we/InfoWeb?p_action=doc&p_docid=0EB59886.

Layden, Tim. Big Foot." *Sports Illustrated*. 30 Dec. 1999. http://vault.sportsillustrated.cnn.com/vault/article/magazine/MAG1017978/index.htm.

---. "Heart and Soul." *Sports Illustrated*. 30 Dec. 1996. http://vault.sportsillustrated.ccn.com/vault/article/magazine/MAG1009291/2/index.htm.

---. "Razing Canes." *Sports Illustrated*. 21 Oct. 1996. http://vault.sportsillustrated.cnn.com/vault/article/magazine/MAG1008912/index.htm.

---. "Seminole Moment." *Sports Illustrated*. 26 Sept. 2005. http://vault.sportsillustrated.cnn.com/vault/article/magazine/MAG1104574/index.htm.

"LeRoy Butler." *Answers.com*. http://www.answers.com/topic/leroy-butler.

Lindley, Mary Ann. "We Almost Saw a Basketball Game Get Rained Out." *Tallahassee Democrat*. 1 Dec. 1994. 1B. http://infoweb.newsbank.com/iw-search/we/InfoWeb?p_action=doc&p_docid=0EB598D7.

Long, Gary. *Stadium Stories: Florida State Seminoles*. Guilford, CN: The

Globe Pequot Press, 2006.

MacArthur, John. *Twelve Ordinary Men.* Nashville: W Publishing Group, 2002.

McDermott, Barry. "The Magic Dragon Is Joust About the Best." *Sports Illustrated.* 25 Sept. 1972. http://vault.sportsillustrated.cc.com/vault/article/magazine/MAG1086565/index.htm.

McGeachy, Ashley. "End Zone Madness." *Sports Illustrated.* 25 Sept. 1995. http://vault.sportsillustrated.cnn.com/vault/article/magazine/MAG 1007152/index.htm.

Milner, Brad. "From War to Lore: Area Players Helped Seminoles Start Football Program." *newsherald.com.* 19 Dec. 2007. http://www.newsherald.com/sports/_2043__article.html/_.html.

Mizell, Hubert. "Peterson Legacy: Coaches." *St. Petersburg Times.* 6 Aug. 1993. 1C. http://pqasb.pqarchiver.com/sptimes/access/51730682.html.

Nogowski, John. "Bowden Finally Has His Trophy." *Tallahassee Democrat.* 3 Jan. 1994. 1A. http://infoweb.newsbank.com/iw-search/we/Info/Web?p_action=doc&p_docid=0EB59889.

---. "Have Mercy? For the Hurricanes? No Way! *Tallahassee Democrat.* 4 Oct. 1997. 1A. http://infoweb.newsbank.com/iw-search/we/Info/Web?p_action=doc&p_docid=0EB599C1.

---. "Martin Stands up for His True FSU Beliefs." *Tallahassee Democrat.* 18 May 1994. 1B. http://infoweb.newsbank.com/iw-search/we/InfoWeb?p_action=doc&p_docid=0EB598AD.

---. "Mientkiewicz, Parents Pull off Happy Ending." *Tallahassee Democrat.* 29 May 1995. 1B. http://infoweb.newsbank.com/iw-search/we/InfoWeb?p_action=doc&p_docid=0EB598FA.

---. "Sura Ignores Call of NBA's Lights to Help Team." *Tallahassee Democrat.* 14 April 1994. 1C. http://infoweb.newsbank.com/iw-search/we/InfoWeb?p_action=doc&p_docid=0EB598A5.

"Our History." *Marching Chiefs: The Largest College Marching Band.* http://www.marchingchiefs.fsu.edu/index.php.

Palermo, Jill. "With Some Field Dressing, FSU Football Players Help Save Student." *Tallahassee Democrat.* 26 Nov. 1996. 1A. http://infoweb.newsbank.com/iw-search/we/InfoWeb?p_action=doc&p_docid=0EB59976.

Putnam, Pat. "Jingle Joints Should Be Judged by His Cover." *Sports Illustrated.* 30 Sept. 1968. http://vault.sportsillustrated.cnn.com/vault/article/magazine/MAG1081639/index.htm.

Redd, Derek. "Florida State Catcher Buster Posey Takes Center Stage." *Palm Beach Post.* 29 May 2008. http://www.palmbeachpost.com/sports/content/sports/epaper/2008/05/29/0530fsu.html.

Reilly, Rick. "A Gentleman and a Scholar." *Sports Illustrated.* 27 Dec. 1993. http://vault.sportsillustrated.cnn.com/vault/article/magazine/MAG1138130/index.htm.

---. "The Road to Victory." *Sports Illustrated.* 5 Sept. 1988. http://vault.sportsillustrated.cnn.com/vault/article/magazine/MAG1067720/2/index.htm.

Schlabach, Mark. *What It Means to Be a Seminole: Bobby Bowden and Florida State's Greatest Players.* Chicago: Triumph Books, 2007.

"Sebastian Janikowski." *JockBio.com.* http://www.jockbio.com/Bios/Janikowski/Janikowski_numbers.html.

Silver, Michael. "Stepping Out." *Sports Illustrated.* 19 May 1997. http://vault.sportsillustrated.cnn.com/vault/article/magazine/MAG1010101/1/index.htm.

Simmons, David Lee. "A Shot Heard All Over: Former Seminole Byron Wells Re-

SEMINOLES

members the Shot Heard Around the Civic Center." *Tallahassee Democrat.* 23 Feb. 1994. 1C. http://info.web/newsbank.com/iw-search/we/InfoWeb? p_action=doc&p_docid=0EB59896.

Sumner, Jim. "Looking Back: 1981 Seminoles Power Through to a National Championship." *TheACC.com.* 9 May 2007. http://www.theacc.com/sports/w-golf/spec-rel/050907aac.html.

"Walter Dix Profile & Bio, Photos & Videos." *2008 Beijing Summer Olympics.* http://www.nbcolympics.com/athletes/athlete=158/bio/index.html.

Yeager, Melanie. "'The Most Wonderful Tradition': FSU's Renegade Celebrates 25th." *Tallahassee Democrat.* 16 Nov. 2002. B1. http://infoweb.newsbank.com/iw-search/we/InfoWeb?p_action=doc&p_docid=0FBE6F15.

INDEX
(LAST NAME, DEVOTION DAY NUMBER)